STIGMA:
A Social
Psychological Analysis

STIGMA:
A Social
Psychological Analysis

IRWIN KATZ
Graduate Center of the City University of New York

LEA LAWRENCE ERLBAUM ASSOCIATES, PUBLISHERS
1981   Hillsdale, New Jersey

Lawrence Erlbaum Associates, Inc., Publishers
365 Broadway
Hillsdale, New Jersey 07642

Library of Congress Cataloging in Publication Data

Katz, Irwin.
    Stigma : a social psychological analysis.

    Bibliography: p.
    Includes index.
    1. Prejudices. 2. Ambivalence. 3. Afro-Americans
—Public opinion. 4. United States—Race relations.
5. Physically handicapped—Public opinion. I. Title.
BF575.P9K37   305   80-20765
ISBN 0-89859-078-7

Printed in the United States of America

To Lois

Contents

Preface

American society's treatment of various minority groups is often ambiguous, even contradictory. Blacks, for example, are protected against job discrimination by Federal laws and regulations that may even require employers to take affirmative action to correct racial imbalances resulting from past bias in hiring practices—yet these same blacks are still excluded from major sectors of the housing market. In the domain of public education, Congress, the courts, and the executive branch have vacillated for over a quarter century on enforcement of the Supreme Court's 1954 ruling against racial segregation in the schools. As regards the physically and mentally handicapped, sweeping Federal legislation that mandates free schooling for all disabled children in the "least restrictive educational environment" was passed in 1975, but the main burden of paying for this ambitious program was left to the already impoverished local school systems.

How do we account for such inconsistencies in public policy toward the disadvantaged? In instances where the civil rights of minority groups have been neglected, their relative lack of political power has no doubt been a factor, particularly when their demands have threatened the interests of the majority. Prejudice also plays a role. To be black or handicapped or very poor is to be marked as inferior and deviant, and therefore undeserving of the same full consideration that is given other people. To the extent that this attitude is held by the electorate, it remains relatively easy for legislators and other public officials to temporize on matters of equal opportunity and the like. Yet in some respects the Government's actions in behalf of minorities seem to go well beyond what would be dictated by purely political considerations. Although generally unpublicized, Federal outlays for antipoverty programs increased substantially during the 1970s, perhaps doubling after the figures are adjusted for inflation. It would seem that, at least in the antipoverty area, norms of social justice and equity have had a strong and continuing influence on this society's responsiveness to the needs of those whom it labels as deviant.

I believe that the incoherence of our national policy toward certain categories of people reflects a corresponding incoherence in the way the majority feel about them. A central thesis of this book is that attitudes about marginal groups are not simply prejudiced, neutral, or accepting, but tend rather to be deeply conflicted and uncertain, a complex mixture of sympathetic and aversive elements. It is further proposed that as a consequence of the ambivalence, behavior toward group members can be erratic and extreme—either in a positive or negative direction depending on how situational factors affect the attitudinal equation. The idea that sentiments about minorities are often conflicted is certainly not new. Erving Goffman (1963) implied as much in his essay on *Stigma,* and much earlier Gunner Myrdal (1944) maintained in *An American Dilemma* that whites' ambivalence about blacks was the key to understanding race relations in this country. But almost no systematic studies were done on this topic prior to the investigations that my colleagues and I carried out. (A few notable exceptions are described later.)

This book describes a program of research on people's reactions to blacks and the physically handicapped, categories that were selected because they seemed to be representative of a whole range of social classes that are generally seen as deviant but also as disadvantaged in their pursuit of life goals. The assumption is that this dual perception generates both hostile and compassionate dispositions. The experiments were designed to evaluate a theory about the conditions under which social contact with a member of a stigmatized group (e.g., a black or a handicapped person) gives rise to extremely favorable or unfavorable behavior toward the person. On the whole, the theory is reasonably well supported by the results, although many unresolved issues remain.

A major portion of the research program was a product of close collaboration between David C. Glass and myself. When we started the project, Dr. Glass was on the faculty of New York University, and I was located at the Graduate Center of the City University of New York. But shortly thereafter, he moved to the University of Texas at Austin, where he remained for a few years. Hence one set of studies was carried out in New York and another set in Austin. (The Austin work is described in Chapter 9.) However, the main theoretical notions, the overall investigative strategy, and the design of key experiments were worked out jointly by Dr. Glass and myself. I assume sole responsibility for the way various concepts are presented in this book, and for whatever weaknesses, errors, or omissions are to be found in its pages.

While other co-investigators have been cited at appropriate places throughout the text, I should like at this time to mention a few whose participation was of special importance. Sheldon Cohen was not only involved in the early experiments but remained interested in the work at all stages and contributed a number of useful insights. David Lucido and Joan Farber, my research assistants, were unstinting in their devotion to the project and an indispensable source of encouragement and stimulation. A number of other people have been helpful by their interest, suggestions, and critical comments at one time or another. In particular, I wish to thank Morton Bard, Howard Ehrlichman, Glen Hass, David Koch, Stanley Milgram, Charles Smith, and Joyce Wackenhut. Saul Podhorzer called my attention to some important sociological writings on ambivalence. The idea for the nonverbal measure of ambivalence (Chapter 10) was provided by Robert Zajonc.

My appreciation goes to Edward E. Jones, who read an earlier version of this manuscript. Dr. Jones made important substantive suggestions that enabled me to improve the book substantially.

To my secretary, Irene Priester, I give sincere thanks for her cheerful forbearance, efficiency, and accurate handling of the manuscript.

I wish gratefully to acknowledge that support for the research was provided by the National Science Foundation (Grants GS-37976X and GS-37977X to myself and Dr. Glass, respectively).

IRWIN KATZ

1 Introduction—
Stigma and Ambivalence

This book is about people's reactions to members of groups that can variously be described as stigmatized, deviant, or of marginal social status. There are many such groups in the United States—blacks; former mental patients; the aged; persons afflicted with physical disabilities, deformities, and chronic diseases; behavioral deviants such as criminals, drug addicts, alcoholics, and prostitutes. Individuals in these categories have attributes that do not accord with prevailing standards of the normal and good. They are often denigrated and avoided— openly in the case of known criminals and other transgressors, or covertly and even unconsciously, as seems to happen when the disdained person is an inno- cent victim of misfortune (e.g., a paraplegic). But apparently under certain conditions, a norm of kindness can strongly influence people's treatment of deviants who are severely deprived, regardless of whether the deprivation was imposed by society or impersonal fate. That is, there is reason to believe that responses to deviancy can be either hostile and rejecting or friendly, sympathetic, and helpful, depending on the circumstances of contact.

In this book I present the results of research that was designed to test a theory about the determinants of positive and negative behavior toward members of socially marginal groups. It is appropriate to begin by discussing two concepts that are of central importance to the theory: *stigma* and *ambivalence*.

THE STIGMA NOTION

To account for the negative, prejudicial side of the majority's reactions to those who are different, social scientists have proposed a whole host of causal factors, some specific to particular minority groups and others more general in their

1

application. What is presently lacking is a single overall perspective for viewing all of these factors in relation to one another. In the interest of such unification, some writers use the term *stigma* to denote the common aspect of all socially disqualifying attributes, however different they may be in other respects. But there is much vagueness in the way the term has been employed. Indeed, Goffman (1963) appears to be the only investigator who has tried to define it explicitly.

Goffman reminds us that the word *stigma* originated with the ancient Greeks, who used it to refer to bodily marks or brands that were designed to expose infamy or disgrace—e.g., that the bearer was a slave or a criminal. Today, Goffman writes, the word is widely used in something like the original literal sense but is applied more to the disgrace itself than to the bodily evidence of it. He prefers to have it denote an attribute that is deeply discrediting—that reduces the possessor in our minds "from a whole and usual person to a tainted, discounted one."[1] Goffman cautions that social context can be crucial; an attribute may be discrediting in one interaction setting but not in another. Nonetheless, there are important attributes that almost everywhere in our society are discrediting.

Some Dimensions of Variation Among Stigmas

To develop an adequate understanding of stigma phenomena, one must take account of the important ways in which stigmas can differ from one another. Three grossly different types of stigma are distinguished by Goffman: "abominations of the body," consisting of various physical deformities, disabilities, and chronic diseases; "blemishes of individual character," which are inferred from a known history of socially deviant behavior; and the inheritable "tribal stigma of race, nation and religion." This of course is not a complete taxonomy, although it seems a useful starting point for thinking about stigma variations and their differential effects on the possessor and the nonstigmatized observer. Goffman does not devote much attention to these differences among stigmas, for his primary intention is to elucidate stigma commonalities and the coping strategies of stigma possessors. The latter concern leads to an interest in distinctions that to some degree crosscut his threefold typology. There is, for example, the distinction between the situation of a person whose stigma is already known to others and that of someone with a concealed stigma. I will consider this and other differences in the stimulus properties of stigmas that seem to determine the extent to which an observer will: (1) be aware of a particular stigma; (2) feel threatened by it; (3) feel sympathy and/or pity for its possessor; and (4) hold the possessor responsible for having it.

---

[1]The process of stigmatization, whereby the perception of a negative attribute in a person becomes associated with global disvaluation of the person, is discussed at length in the Appendix.

Visibility and Related Variables. Goffman (1963), being interested in the strategies for impression management that are used by the stigmatized, discusses at some length the visibility aspect of stigmas. By this he means not just visual perceptibility but the general "evidentness" of a stimulus, which he distinguishes from three other notions that he feels are often confused with it. The first he calls the "known-aboutness" of the attribute—whether others know about the individual's stigma may be based not on current visibility but on whether they have previous knowledge about him, derived perhaps from gossip or a previous contact with the person when the stigma was visible. The next feature to be distinguished from visibility is that of obtrusiveness—the extent to which a stigma interferes with the flow of interaction. For instance, the blind person's cane is a very visible symbol but it can be disattended, but his failure to direct his face to the eyes of conversational co-participants repeatedly disrupts the feedback mechanics of spoken interaction. The third factor is the perceived focus of a stigma. This refers to the normal person's perception of the sphere of life activity for which the particular attribute disqualifies the possessor. Thus ugliness is a stigma that is focused in social situations; it ought to have no effect on the person's competency in solitary tasks. A diabetic condition, on the other hand, may have no effect on the person's qualifications for face-to-face interaction but may lead to discrimination in employment. All of these factors determine people's levels of awareness of a particular stigma in various interaction situations, hence the extent to which they will treat the possessors as deviant.

Threat. Most stigmas probably hold an element of threat for people who are exposed to them, but the kind and severity of threat seem to vary greatly among different stigmas. Behavioral deviants such as criminals, delinquents, political radicals, and religious cultists challenge basic societal values and assumptions. Some of these groups may also elicit fears of physical harm and social disorder. Racial minorities are sometimes perceived by whites as dangerous competitors for jobs, housing, and community resources.

Interactions with the sick and injured may, for a variety of reasons, arouse apprehensiveness in normals. The contact may cast doubt on the widely held belief that the world is a just place where the innocent do not suffer (Lerner, 1970), remind the normal person of his vulnerability to sudden misfortune, or raise the prospect of becoming enmeshed in another person's dependency. Moreover, to the extent that these factors lead to avoidance of someone who is disabled, the normal actor may experience a lowering of self-esteem. Those who have conditions that are severe and permanent, then, would pose a greater threat to well people than would those with mild, curable conditions. Also, disorders that are mysterious and relatively uncontrollable (e.g., cancer) seem to be more threatening and more stigmatizing than conditions that are just as dangerous but are thought to be better understood medically (e.g., heart disease). Within the realm of mental or emotional illness, there should be variations in the threat value of conditions, relating to differences in behavioral manifestations and potential reversibility. Thus neurotic anxiety sufferers, who are often outwardly nervous and unpredictable, should be more threatening to other people than are depressives, whose behavior may be subdued and nondisruptive.

Such variations as have just been mentioned in the threat potential of stigmas should engender differential levels of fear and hostility on the part of the non-stigmatized.

Sympathy Arousal.   By definition, to be stigmatized is to be deprived by society. But people's reactions to members of deviant groups are not always negative. One can also discern feelings of sympathy for the underdog, distress over another's suffering, even respect for those who strive to overcome severe handicaps. Thus there is a strong social norm in this country that the physically and mentally disabled should be treated well, a norm that finds concrete expression in a vast network of public and private helping agencies. However, specific types of deprivation are not always apparent to outsiders.

For instance, there is probably a more widespread awareness of job discrimination against blacks and women than against former mental patients, even though the latter may actually be subjected to as much or more negative bias. Stigmas also differ in the extent to which they are perceived as being intrinsically disabling. For example, a physical handicap will likely be regarded as more incapacitating than a prison record. Further, the perception of physical disability will to a large extent depend on the visibility of the handicap, which in turn may sometimes be determined by the ability of the audience to decode disability cues. As a result of the civil rights activities of various minority groups during the 1960s and 1970s, society in general is much more aware of their special problems than it had been earlier. One may assume that the more evident a particular group's disadvantages, the more likely that others will feel sympathy for its members and want to help them. But it also appears to be true, as Heider (1958) and others have noted, that deprivation is often taken as a sign of badness and guilt. It has been commonly observed through the ages that poverty and weakness evoke negative evaluations, even contempt.

Perceived Responsibility.   Stigmas differ in the extent to which the possessor is likely to be held responsible by judges for his or her deviance. Goffman's (1963) characterological stigmas, entailing known or alleged violations of moral norms, would no doubt tend to be viewed (at least on a conscious level) as more voluntary than the tribal and bodily stigmas. But even among the latter types, there should be differences in the tendency to attribute responsibility for having a deviant characteristic. Thus some physical conditions are more likely to be seen as resulting from negligence, self-indulgence, or immorality than are others. Negative attitudes about the obese, for example, are tied to the belief that they could control their weight if they really wanted to. There may also be a relatively primitive, unconscious tendency to assign more blame to handicapped individuals when the disorder is genetically determined than when it is the result of an accident, since the former type of causation may be perceived as more closely associated with the person. Similarly, with respect to emotional or mental disorders, there is probably less culpability ascribed to someone suffering from reactive depression brought on by the loss of a loved one, menopause, etc., than to the victim of an inexplicable, endogenous depression. Whether the individual is or is not blamed for possessing a deviant trait will likely have important consequences for the way he is treated.

Implication of the Foregoing.   Consideration of the stimulus properties just mentioned suggests that many types of marginal individuals may be perceived not only as *deviant*—i.e., as deeply faulted human beings—but also as *disadvantaged*—either by the disabling nature of their distinctive characteristic (as in the case of blindness, chronic illness, inherited poverty), by the social and economic discrimination that having it entails, or by both factors. It stands to reason that this dual perspective will engender in observers contradictory feelings of antipathy and compassion about the object. That ambivalence is a fundamental feature of people's attitudes toward a range of stigmatized groups is an assumption that has guided the research to be presented in later chapters.

AMBIVALENCE

Bleuler (1910) coined the term *ambivalence* to refer to various kinds of psychic conflict: (1) emotional, i.e., oscillation between love and hate; (2) voluntary, i.e., inability to decide on an action; and (3) intellectual, i.e., belief in contradictory propositions. In psychoanalytic writings, the term is generally used in the first of these senses. Thus Freud (1923/1961) stated, "Now, clinical observation shows not only that love is with unexpected regularity accompanied by hate (ambivalence), and not only that in human relationships hate is frequently a forerunner of love, but also that in a number of circumstances hate changes into love and love into hate [p. 42]." For Freud, ambivalence was a "fundamental phenomenon" representing an incomplete fusion of two classes of instincts, "the sexual instincts of Eros" (which included love), and a death, or destruction, instinct, manifested as hate.[2]

---

[2]The affective reversibility of human relationships was noted by the ancient Greeks, as in these lines by Sophocles (1938):

Of all men I, whom proof has taught too late
How so far only should we hate our foes
As though we soon might love them, and so far
Do a friend a service, as to one most like

Discussions of ambivalence are not confined to the clinical literature. Indeed, several sociologists and social psychologists have viewed ambivalence as a central feature of social interactions. Simmel (1908/1956) believed that the operation of polar opposite tendencies between people was essential to the life of any social unit. "Just as the universe needs 'love and hate,'" he observed, "that is, attractive and repulsive forces, in order to have any form at all, so society too, in order to attain a determinate shape, needs some quantitative ratio of harmony and disharmony, of association and competition, of favorable and unfavorable tendencies [p. 15]." Simmel suggested that in early cultural periods these opposing social currents were clearly separated, but as a culture matured, complex relations between persons were more often found—relations that had their roots "in a twilight condition of feeling whose outcome might be hatred almost as easily as love, or whose undifferentiated character is even sometimes betrayed by oscillations between the two [p. 25]."[3] Hostility and sympathy were seen by Simmel as the natural bases or forms of human relations, the two often appearing side by side—as manifested, for instance, in the "strange lively interest... which people usually show in the suffering of others [p. 28]."

In this regard, Rapoport (1974) distinguished between callousness, or indifference, and cruelty, which he saw as closely related to sympathy. Callousness reflected a lack of identification with those who suffer; cruelty, on the contrary, was evidence of identification with the sufferer—but with a negative "sign," as it were. That is, "Cruelty is the property of deriving pleasure from the suffering of others, just as empathy is sharing the suffering of others or of experiencing distress from the suffering of others [p. 121]." For Rapoport, then, both cruelty and empathy presupposed identification with the object of brutality or of compassion. They were two sides of the same coin. Rapoport regarded as ambivalent not only this ability to imagine how the other feels, but all specifically human faculties.

Another source of duality in human relationships was described by Angyal (1941) in his distinction between two very general tendencies of the organism. One is the urge toward autonomy, or self-determination, toward mastering oneself and the environment; the other is the trend toward homonomy, a trend to fuse and be in harmony with superindividual units, to be in accord with forces from the outside that impinge upon the person. The drive for autonomy gives rise to

---

Some day to prove our foe; since oftenest men
In friendship but a faithless haven find [p. 336].

In modern literature, the following lines from Yeats (1949) suggest a natural affinity between love and hate:

Come near, that no more blinded by man's fate,
I find under the boughs of love and hate,
In all poor foolish things that live a day,
Eternal beauty wandering on her way [p. 35].

[3]In contrast to Simmel's view, Freud (1913/1953) believed that the "psychical impulses of primitive peoples were characterized by a higher amount of ambivalence than is to be found in modern civilized man. It is to be supposed that as this ambivalence diminished, taboo slowly disappeared [p. 66]."

aggression, whereas the drive for homonomy generates an opposite urge to unite with other people in harmony. Opposing impulses could also arise from the perception of power and weakness, according to Heider (1958). People in general admire strength or power and despise weakness and impotence; but there is also an opposite tendency. Power may engender suspicion and hostility, and weakness may lead to positive sentiments. There may even be an inborn love of the helpless.

Cuber (1963) noted that ambivalence often springs from the conflicts between the attitudes a person actually acquires through his unique experience and the attitudes he is supposed to have acquired according to the norms of his culture. Cuber saw most individuals resolving the ambivalent conflict in some measure by behaving overtly in the manner in which they are expected and keeping their disapproving attitudes to themselves. "This does not entirely solve the problem, of course, because some people are sensitive to being 'hypocrites' and may have mental conflicts resulting from such 'insincerities.' The chief point to be noted here, however, is the normality and inevitability of ambivalence for many persons in many situations [p. 279]."

The overt expression of ambivalence may create friction within social relationships because it is a display of gross inconsistencies in a person's self-presentation. Certain sociologists and ethnomethodologists (Garfinkel, 1964; Goffman, 1959) have stressed the importance of consistent self-presentations in social interactions. Smooth social encounters are governed by presentations of self that are consistent with the expectations and the assumptions of the participants. A profuse display of ambivalent emotions, attitudes, or behaviors would certainly disrupt the "working consensus" of the participants and would create conflicts in their "definition of the situation." As Cuber suggested, a person can maintain a consistent self-presentation while harboring an ambivalent conflict if one side of the ambivalence is publicly expressed while the other side is experienced privately. This can easily be achieved by what Goffman (1959) has termed the presentation of a "false front." The deceptive nature of false fronts may at times be quite ambiguous because "the performer can be fully taken in by his own act; he can be sincerely convinced that the impression of reality which he stages is the real reality [p. 17]."

How Ambivalence Is Experienced

Although the research to be presented in later chapters does not deal directly with the phenomenology of ambivalence, this discussion would be incomplete without at least a brief reference to the topic. Very little descriptive material is to be found in the psychological literature on how ambivalence is represented in consciousness. But the following preliminary generalizations strike me as able. To begin, it seems that people often are unaware of their toward others, or at least are unaware of the full intensity of the conflict. And since hostility is more apt than liking to be disapproved of by society, it probably is usually the negative side of the attitudinal equation that is not fully present in awareness. Ambivalence is sometimes experienced indirectly, e.g., as blocked behavior. This can be illustrated by a small example from a work of fiction. In Lawrence's *Sons and Lovers* (1913/1969), Mrs. Morel at one point was only dimly cognizant of her growing distaste for her husband, which she experienced as inhibition. When he approached her, "She half wanted him to kiss her, but could not bring herself to give any sign. She only breathed freely when he was gone out of the room again . . . [p. 33]." When ambivalence enters consciousness more directly, it probably tends to be experienced as an alternation of positive and negative feelings, as a function of changing situational cues and other momentary determinants. It seems unlikely that opposite emotions are characteristically experienced at the same time, although something approaching this phenomenon may occur under extreme conditions.

It is my belief that much can be learned about the nature of emotional experience from stories and novels, even though the best of these works must be regarded as imaginative rather than reportorial in intent. There is, for example, an episode in *The Brothers Karamazov* in which Dostoievsky (no date) traces vividly and in subtle detail the mind processes of a person tormented by love and hate [p. 121ff.]. Dimitri Karamazov, the corrupt sensualist, confesses to his brother, Alyosha, how he tried to humiliate Katerina Ivanovna, to whom he was strongly attracted, because she had spurned him. He had enticed her to his apartment with a promise to provide the funds needed to save her father from financial ruin and disgrace. She arrived "breathless, frightened, her voice failed her, and the corners of her mouth and the lines round it quivered . . . ." He experienced intense guilt ("Well, I felt a centipede biting my heart—a noxious insect . . . ") and then (as shown in the following passage) in rapid sequence, admiration for his intended victim, self-loathing, an ecstasy of triumphant hatred. Dimitri says:

> I looked her up and down, You've seen her? She's a beauty. But she was beautiful in a different way then. At that moment she was beautiful because she was noble, and I was a scoundrel; she in all the grandeur of her generosity and sacrifice for her father, and I—a bug! And, scoundrel as I was, she was altogether at my mercy, body and soul . . . I tell you frankly, that . . . venomous thought so possessed my heart that it almost swooned with suspense. It seemed as if there could be no resisting it, as though I should act like a bug, like a venomous spider, without a spark of pity. I could scarcely breath [p. 112].

The thought crossed Dimitri's mind that if he were to seduce Katerina and then offer marriage she would undoubtedly still spurn him. This enraged him, and he spitefully "longed to play her the nastiest, swinish cad's trick"—to seduce her and then not give her the money she needed to save her father. But he knew he would "have howled with regret all the rest of my life." Then he looked at her "... for three seconds, or five perhaps, with fearful hatred—that hate which is only a hair's-breadth from love, from the maddest love!" He experienced a physical sensation that symbolized the unity of opposites in this complex love-hate emotion. In Dimitri's words, "I went to the window, put my forehead against the frozen pane, and I remember the ice burnt my forehead like fire." He turned round, got the money from the table, and gave it to Katerina in silence. Next he opened the door for her to leave, "... and, stepping back, made her a deep bow, a most respectful, a most impressive bow, believe me!" She "shuddered all over with fright and relief," returned his bow, touching her forehead to the floor, then jumped up and ran away. Dimitri, now alone, performed an act that symbolized his inner turmoil. He drew his sword and nearly stabbed himself, "... why, I don't know. It would have been frightfully stupid, of course. I suppose it was from delight ... But I didn't stab myself. I only kissed my sword and put it back in the scabbard."

One must of course be cautious about accepting the foregoing as a valid account of conscious processes. For one thing, Dostoievsky's intention was probably more esthetic than scientific. For another, Dimitri's account of the episode cannot be assumed to be free of memory errors or self-serving distortions and embellishments. But granting these points, one is still struck by the verisimilitude of the narrative and by its psychological suggestiveness. It is noteworthy that in this particular episode, as described, the flow of Dimitri's conscious thoughts and feelings is little influenced by changes in the situation. Katerina's behavior does not enter into the account from the time she appears until just before she leaves; the cues that trigger Dimitri's rapidly shifting reactions are mostly internal, one conscious content giving rise to another. Also, positive and negative affects seem to be experienced both successively and simultaneously, but in the latter case in a confused, undifferentiated way. The clearest representations of simultaneous duality of feeling seem to be symbolic, as in Dimitri's sensation of fire and ice when his forehead touches the window pane and in his abortive act of joyous self-injury.

Research Relating to Ambivalence

An illuminating series of studies were carried out by Miller (1959) and his co-workers, in which ambivalence was construed essentially as an expression of an approach-avoidance conflict.[4] In the experimental paradigm employed by these investigators, separate gradients for the tendencies to approach and avoid a goal region were plotted. This was done by exposing organisms (laboratory rats) to either an attractive or aversive stimulus (food or an electrified grid) in the same place and then observing their behaviors when placed at various distances

---

[4]Miller's analysis is similar to an earlier conceptualization of the approach-avoidance conflict situation by Lewin (1935).

from the critical area. From a knowledge of the respective gradients, it was possible to predict that animals exposed to *both* types of stimulus (food plus shocks) in the critical area would show an oscillation between approach and avoidance when placed near the area. This research is informative about the motivational components of approach–avoidance conflict. But obviously it does not deal with certain important symbolic aspects of ambivalence in human relationships. For example, should the individual with conflicted feelings about another person perceive his own behavior as insincere or inconsistent, he may experience a threat to self-esteem that could generate various defensive reactions. A frequent type of defense, according to the psychoanalytic literature, involves the suppression of one side of the ambivalent equation and enhancement of the other side, so that overt treatment of the attitudinal object becomes either extremely positive or negative. Miller's theoretical model does not refer to these processes.

Except for the work of Miller and his associates, there has been virtually no experimental research on ambivalence. One possible cause of the neglect is the fact that investigations of social interactions have generally been governed by the implicit assumption that there is a single dimension of like–dislike. This influence is apparent in the choice of measuring instruments. One of the most widely used techniques for assessing sentiments is the semantic differential questionnaire devised by Osgood, Suci, and Tannenbaum (1957), which is based on the notion that one's evaluation of any person or group can be assessed by means of a set of bipolar rating scales (e.g., good–bad, dirty–clean, cruel–kind), where the midpoint of the scale represents neutrality. Osgood et al. rule out the possibility that an object might be perceived as *both* good and bad, etc., so that a response at the midpoint would reflect attitudinal conflict instead of indifference. Another method of assessing feelings about another person, developed by Byrne (1971), has been used in numerous studies of interpersonal attraction. It consists of two closely correlated rating scales that ask the subject to indicate how much he likes the other and whether he believes he would enjoy or dislike working with him. The measure of attraction is the sum of the ratings on the respective scales. Clearly, the use of this instrument more or less guarantees that any ambivalence the subject may have about the stimulus person will remain concealed. Another area of research that has been strongly influenced by the assumption of a single like–dislike dimension is that of impression formation. In their review of this topic, Kanouse and Hanson (1971) point out that the assumption underlies two of the main theories about how incoming information about a stranger is processed—the adding and averaging models.

However, there is reason to believe that the single-dimension notion is invalid. Thus Kaplan (1972) has shown that when the bipolar evaluative scales of the semantic differential technique are split into unipolar scales, subjects' separate ratings of positive traits and their negative opposites show a considerable amount of independence from each other. This suggests a potential for ambivalence. Also, Miller's (1959) demonstration that there exist different gradients of approach and avoidance logically implies independent approach and avoidance tendencies. And from another perspective, Stein (1964) and Cantril (1967) have argued that there are separate and relatively independent reward and punishment systems in the brain. If two distinct and independent systems are involved in the evaluation of compound stimuli, there is reason to assume that positive and negative feelings toward an object can exist simultaneously or in oscillation. A similar conclusion is reached by Kanouse and Hanson (1971), who quote Jordan (1965) to the effect that the custom of finding an arithmetic average of attitude ratings that includes both positive and negative ratings may be "a mixing of apples and cabbages."[5]

FOCUS OF THIS BOOK

As mentioned earlier, a central assumption of this book is that attitudes toward many deviant groups tend to be ambivalent rather than simply hostile or accepting. The studies to be reported explore some of the behavioral implications of this assumption. They were designed to evaluate a theory about the ways in which most people try to resolve inner conflicts that are aroused during social interactions with deviant individuals. As part of the overall research strategy, predictions from the theory are usually tested with two types of stimulus persons—blacks and the physically handicapped. These groups are very different from each other yet share a common fate of being stigmatized by the dominant society in the United States. Therefore, it seemed that if similar reactions on the part of nonstigmatized subjects toward blacks and the handicapped could be demonstrated, and these reactions were in accord with the proposed theory, there would be credible evidence of the theory's applicability to stigma phenomena in general.

---

[5]I do not mean to imply that ambivalence can be adequately conceptualized as a simple, symmetrical opposition between positive and negative cognitive-affective components. The theoretical and empirical material presented in this chapter and in Chapter 2 indicates that positive effects, being more likely to have social approval, tend to be more conscious, verbal, and openly expressed than negative effects. Regarding reactions to minority groups such as blacks and the physically handicapped, socialization encourages the expression of egalitarian, friendly sentiments and the suppression of hostile, subordinating attitudes. Hence the negative beliefs and feelings tend to be more unconscious and covert, their expression in some way inhibited by the positive ones. That is, positive and negative are not simply conflicting forces with comparable dynamics aimed in different directions. It would follow from this that the negative attitudes should be tapped more readily by more private or indirect response measures—such as projective tests, indices of nonverbal behavior, and unobtrusive observation of social interaction—whereas positive feelings should be more prominent when the response is public and evaluation apprehension becomes an obvious factor. These issues become crucial in later chapters when different response measures are found to yield discrepant information about subjects' reactions to stigmatized stimulus persons.

In Chapter 2, I review the empirical support from previous studies for the view that the majority's feelings and beliefs about blacks and the disabled tend to be ambivalent. Chapter 3 presents the theory that has been formulated to account for overt behavior toward stigmatized stimulus persons. In Chapters 4 through 10, the relevant research is described. And Chapter 11 deals with the implications of the results and some additional issues pertaining to stigma processes.

2 Attitudes Toward Blacks and the Handicapped

In this country blacks are negatively stereotyped and segregated, whereas the blind, deaf, and crippled are usually regarded as unfortunate people who may legitimately expect help from others. It is also true, although less widely recognized, that these dominant dispositions of prejudice against blacks and sympathy for the handicapped are often accompanied by feelings of an opposite kind—that is, of friendliness toward blacks and aversion for the handicapped. Thus it has been observed that most whites are concerned about the existence of racial inequality and discrimination and that the physically impaired are frequently patronized or avoided. Evidence is presented that tends to support the view that ambivalence is an important feature of attitudes toward both of these groups.

ATTITUDES ABOUT BLACKS

In his classic study of race relations in the United States, Myrdal (1944) made the provocative suggestion that inner conflict and guilt are fundamental elements in white America's racial outlook—that the contradiction between the egalitarian precepts of the democratic creed and existing segregationist practices poses a moral dilemma for the dominant majority, which is the key to understanding black–white relationships.[1] Although Myrdal's thesis stimulated lively debate among social scientists, there has been relatively little research specifically

[1]This is Myrdal's (1944) eloquent statement of the issue:

The American Negro problem is a problem in the heart of the American. It is there that the interracial tension has its focus. It is there that the decisive struggle goes on. This is the central viewpoint of this treatise. Though our study includes economic, social, and political race relations, at bottom our problem is the moral dilemma of the American—the conflict between his moral valuations on various levels of

13

designed to test its two main propositions—namely, that: (1) most whites have value-attitude systems that are fundamentally inconsistent as they pertain to racial matters; and (2) the inconsistency makes for moral uneasiness. However, national opinion surveys and other attitudinal studies provide some support for the dilemma theory.

There is a consistent pattern of findings in the opinion polls of the past 15 years: Most whites acknowledge that nonwhites are discriminated against and endorse general goals associated with racial integration and racial equality but continue to resist strongly many types of specific reform. For example, Brink and Harris (1964) reported that fully 71% of a nation-wide white adult sample, and even 56% of a southern sample, said they believed that blacks were treated unfairly. Substantial majorities felt that there was racial discrimination in jobs, housing, and education. Brink and Harris observed that "when whites were asked how they thought it must feel to be discriminated against as a Negro, they bristled with indignation and even outrage at the thought of being treated like a Negro [p. 147]." Yet questions about specific integration measures elicited strong resistance. According to the investigators, the prevailing view among whites was clearly that blacks were pressing too hard, asking for too much. Two years later, Brink and Harris (1966) found that 70% of white respondents thought blacks were trying to move too fast.

In Angus Campbell's (1971) survey of white attitudes in 15 major cities, 56% felt that in their communities there was racial discrimination in job hiring and promotion, and 67% favored legislation against such practices. Yet when asked if the inferior socioeconomic status of blacks was "due mainly to Negros being discriminated against, or mainly to something about Negroes themselves," 56% attributed their inferior status mainly to blacks themselves, 19% to "a mixture of both," and only 19% mainly to discrimination. "Most commonly," wrote Campbell, "the 'something' they have in mind is what they take to be the Negro's lack of ambition, laziness, failure to take advantage of his opportunities [p. 14]." From the replies on these and other questions, Campbell concluded that a substantial proportion of urban whites—perhaps half—had racial perceptions, feelings, and beliefs that were ambiguous and conflicted.

A more recent study, conducted by *The New York Times* (Herbers, 1978), indicates that whites in the urban North are now more accepting of black neighbors and co-workers than they were in the 1960s but have little interest in knowing about contemporary problems of racial inequality. Respondents tended to over-

---

consciousness and generality. The "American Dilemma," referred to in the title of this book, is the ever-raging conflict between, on the one hand, the valuations preserved on the general plane which we call the "American Creed," where the American thinks, talks, and acts under the influence of high national and Christian precepts, and, on the other hand, the valuations on specific planes of individual and group living, where personal and local interests; economic, social, and sexual jealousies; considerations of community prestige and conformity; group prejudice against particular persons or types of people; and all sorts of miscellaneous wants, impulses, and habits dominate his outlook [p. xliii].

estimate the civil rights gains of recent years, to see little need for additional anti-discrimination measures.

Another type of evidence of ambivalence is provided by studies that employed psychometric scales. Woodmansee and Cook (1967) obtained generally large intercorrelations among 10 racial prejudice subscales that they developed by means of factor analysis, but negligible correlations between these subscales and a measure of sympathetic identification with blacks. Hence a sizeable proportion of their total sample must have held inconsistent racial attitudes in the sense of being both sympathetic and prejudiced. Similarly, Kaplan (1972), using an attitude measurement technique that divides the bipolar scales of Osgood's semantic differential into separate unipolar scales, found that subjects' "liking" responses toward a given ethnic group (i.e., ascriptions of positive qualities such as "good," "wise," and "clean") were relatively independent of their "disliking" responses (i.e., ascriptions of negative qualities such as "bad," "foolish," and "dirty").

The findings just reviewed suggest that members of the dominant group tend to have racial orientations that are inconsistent, but it is left unclear whether the inconsistency is (as Myrdal contended) a source of moral discomfort. A few strands of evidence bearing on this question are provided by studies that have examined the relationship between whites' general values and their civil rights views. Ernest Campbell (1961) observed that the views on racial integration that southern white college students thought they ought to have were much more liberal than the ones they admitted actually having. Unfortunately, the investigator did not try to probe the extent of subjects' uneasiness over the discrepancies. This was done by Westie (1965). He found white northerners more liberal in their general democratic values than in their stands on specific civil rights issues; he also noted that in the course of being interviewed, most individuals recognized the inconsistencies spontaneously, and many even manifested considerable anxiety when the contradictions became apparent to them. Similarly, Allport (1954) reported that in a sample of college essays on personal experiences with minority groups, only about 10% of the students who had experienced prejudice did so without betraying feelings of guilt and conflict.

Perhaps the clearest demonstration of how awareness of racial-attitude inconsistency can create psychic tension and even change behavior is to be found in Rokeach's (1973) experiments on self-confrontation. College students were made aware of discrepancies between their avowed personal values and their position on civil rights issues. For example, subjects typically ranked the value freedom much higher than the value equality. They were told that this indicated they were more interested in their own freedom than they were in freedom for other people. Many were shown discrepancies between their high ranking of freedom and their lukewarm endorsement of equal rights for blacks. Rokeach found that this procedure engendered self-dissatisfaction in subjects, which in turn led to an increase in pro-black actions. For example, several months later more than twice as many experimental subjects as control subjects responded to a mail solicitation from the National Association for the Advancement of Colored People by joining the organization.[2]

Another type of experimental approach to the Myrdalian conflict model was used by Weitz (1972). Her study dealt with the relationship between verbal attitudes toward blacks and unobtrusive measures of behavior. White college males were placed in a simulated interracial encounter in which they expected to interact with a black or white stimulus person. A general pattern of conflicting responses to minority targets was found—of overt friendliness and covert rejection. Favorableness of subjects' impression ratings of the blacks was negatively related to friendliness of: (1) voice tone; and (2) behavior directed toward them; while voice tone was positively related to behavior. Weitz saw these results as suggesting that many individuals overreacted to the social norm of verbal acceptance of blacks, possibly due to repression of negative affect, and hence were likely to be unconsciously opposed to actual interracial contact.

Overall, then, there is suggestive evidence that white people often have conflicted sentiments and beliefs relating to racial matters and that feelings of unease are experienced when the conflicts are made salient. Sympathy for the underdog and commitment to a norm of justice appear to be important positive components of the dominant group's racial outlook, whereas a variety of fears and derogatory beliefs are found on the negative side.[3] The 1970s witnessed the polarization of the black urban population into two segments: one relatively prosperous and upwardly mobile, the other very poor, underemployed, and increasingly alienated from the main society. Whites tend to associate the latter element with most of today's urban ills, such as street crime, high welfare costs, and physical decay; but the former group is also perceived as threatening—as dangerous competitors for jobs, housing, and educational resources (cf. Ashmore & DelBoca, 1976).

ATTITUDES ABOUT THE DISABLED

Although there are many speculative theories and opinions about the nature of attitudes toward the sick and disabled, systematic research on this topic has been meager. Some studies have assessed the majority's reactions to the physically

---

[2]Rosenberg's (1960) hypnosis study and McGuire's (1960) belief percolation effect studies provide further evidence of the tension-producing properties of cognitive inconsistency. In these investigations, induced change in one part of an attitudinal structure brought about far-reaching realignments throughout the structure.

[3]The extraordinary popularity of Alex Haley's (1976) book, *Roots,* and of the eight-part television dramatization of this account of his search for his African ancestry, is not readily explainable except as an expression of the white majority's friendly interest in black Americans. The book was on the national best seller list for over a year, and some 130 million people watched at least part of the television series. Indeed, the last episode had over 80 million viewers, an all-time record. Although the shows had some of the familiar ingredients of successful TV melodrama, conventional entertainment values can hardly account for their exceptional appeal to a predominantly white audience.

handicapped by means of interviews and questionnaires, and a few have involved observations of overt behavior. However, the bulk of information about attitudes toward the disabled has been gleaned from classical and modern literature, religious writings, folklore, popular humor, and personal accounts by handicapped informants. Whatever the source of information, these attitudes are usually found to be a mixture of positive and negative elements.

Considering first the favorable feelings and beliefs, it hardly needs documentation that kindly treatment of the handicapped is socially approved and that indifference to their plight is considered reprehensible. This norm is based on Judeo-Christian teachings (Barker, Wright, Meyerson, & Gonick, 1953). The New Testament states that disease may be a means of purification and a way of grace. Suffering perfects the sufferer. Accordingly, the sick have a preferential position, and it is a privilege for the healthy to minister to them. At the heart of this doctrine is the image of Christ the Healer as an ideal model of devotion to the physically afflicted.

Friendliness and compassion are supported by the belief, apparently widely held, that wisdom and deep understanding emerge from suffering (Crutchfield, 1955; Dembo, 1953). In the same vein, Wright (1960) points out that people are inclined to respect those who manage to cope with adversity. Since many who are crippled or deformed seem to adjust to their loss, to arrange their lives in accordance with their abilities and opportunities, it is to be expected that evaluations of these groups will often be favorable. In fact, several questionnaire studies have found that most adults tend to assign positive traits to the disabled. For example, when Mussen and Barker (1944) asked college students to rate the orthopedically impaired on 24 personality characteristics, cripples as compared with noncripples were described as more conscientious, self-reliant, kind, persistent, intelligent, original, unselfish, and religious. The former received relatively unfavorable ratings on only two traits: They were seen as somewhat overly sensitive and as lacking in social adaptibility. Predominantly positive ratings of handicapped people have also been reported by Strong (1931), Ray (1946), and Kleck (1968).[4]

Whereas public, verbalized attitudes about those who have bodily defects are on the average favorable, deeper, largely unconscious feelings are often rejecting (cf. Barker et al., 1953; Goffman, 1963; Hentig, 1948; Safilios-Rothschild, 1970; Wright, 1960). There is evidence of a general desire to avoid these individuals (e.g., Kleck, 1968; Kleck, Ono, & Hastorf, 1966; Piliavin, Piliavin, & Robin, 1975; Shears & Jensema, 1969; Snyder, Kleck, Strenta, & Mentzer, 1979; Tringo, 1970). In Tringo's study, high school, college, and graduate students, and health-care workers were given a questionnaire that tapped willing-

---

[4]But several studies of children have revealed predominantly *negative* reactions to handicapped age peers (e.g., Richardson, 1970, 1971; Richardson & Royce, 1968). These attitudes become more favorable as the children get older (Gozali, 1971).

ness to enter into relationships of various degrees of intimacy with persons having different types of chronic illness and disability. Of 22 target groups, every one was rejected to some extent, with the following being unacceptable even as next door neighbors: cerebral palsy sufferers, epileptics, paraplegics, dwarfs, hunchbacks. Sufferers from only a few relatively minor illnesses were acceptable as a relative (other than spouse) through marriage.[5]

Further evidence of prejudice against the disabled is to be found in their descriptions of encounters with other persons. In a host of written and oral accounts, the theme of being pitied, subordinated, and ignored is expressed again and again (reviewed by Barker et al., 1953; Goffman, 1963; Wright, 1960). Consider, for example, the following excerpt (Carling, 1962):

> I also learned that the cripple must be careful not to act differently from what people expect him to do. Above all they expect the cripple to be crippled; to be disabled and helpless; to be inferior to themselves, and they will become suspicious and insecure if the cripple falls short of these expectations [p. 54].

Additional documentation is provided by content analyses of cultural products. Barker et al. made a survey of the frequency of jokes about persons with physical defects. In five collections of jokes that included several thousand items, 4.1% of the jokes were concerned with the disabled, who were clearly deprecated 80% of the time. By way of comparison, jokes about farmers, salesmen, judges, and dentists were deprecatory about half as often. The same authors summarized studies of the treatment of the blind in fiction and found agreement that the idealized and abnormally good blind person was the most frequent stereotype but that the repugnant and abnormally bad character was not infrequent. The normal, well-adjusted blind person was rarely encountered.

Certainly the association of physical abnormality with moral taint is as deeply ingrained in Western culture as is the compassionate view. The ancient Greeks

---

[5]The relationship between degree of intimacy and reactions to physical and other types of stigma is complex. Although, in general, familiarity with the physically or psychologically handicapped tends to break down stereotypes and promote greater understanding and acceptance, there probably are numerous circumstances in which increased social contact will have a negative effect on the attitudes of the nonhandicapped. Referring to relationships between disabled individuals and family members or other intimates, Goffman (1963) points out that those who are obliged to be in full contact with the person may find it more difficult to accept him than those who are not required to share his stigma or spend much time exerting tact and care in regard to it. Also, some bodily or behavioral conditions can be concealed from strangers and mere acquaintances with relative ease, and have their effect chiefly on intimates. Goffman concludes:

> Instead, then, of thinking of a continuum of relationships, with categoric and concealing treatment at one end and particularistic, open treatment at the other, it might be better to think of various structures in which contact occurs and is stabilized—public streets and their strangers, perfunctory service relations, the workplace, the neighborhood, the domestic scene—and to see that in each case characteristic discrepancies are likely to occur between virtual and actual social identity, and characteristic efforts are made to manage the situation [p. 55].

explained disease most often as an instrument of divine wrath; it could be a punishment for a personal fault, a collective transgression, or a crime of one's ancestors (Sontag, 1978). The Old Testament enumerates 12 afflictions that disqualified a priest from officiating, including blindness, lameness, and a variety of facial and bodily disfigurements. It is strictly commanded that "the blind and the lame shall not come into the house" (quoted by Hentig, 1948). Until well into modern times, the superstition persisted in Europe that the deformed were works of the Devil (McDaniel, 1969). Even Martin Luther believed in the theory of the "changeling"—that cripples were substituted for real children by the Devil and that if the crippled were maltreated enough the diabolical mother would return the real child.

The punitive fantasies and myths concocted around certain frightful illnesses have been written about by Sontag (1978), who makes the point that in the twentieth century cancer has taken on a moral significance comparable to that of leprosy in the Middle Ages. Cancer is regarded as not just a lethal disease but a shameful one, a symbol of corruption and decay. It arouses a disproportionate sense of horror, an irrational dread of contamination. Sontag's thesis is supported by recent empirical findings. For instance, Severo (1977) reports that the feelings of people toward friends and relatives who have cancer emerge frequently as brittle and ugly; initial feelings and expressions of sympathy often give way to anger and resentment. In a comprehensive review of research on social psychological aspects of cancer, Wortman and Dunkel-Schetter (1979) refer to people's "ambivalence, confusion and discomfort" in social contacts with cancer patients. They state, "There is considerable evidence that people avoid cancer patients, that they discourage open communication with the patient, and that they give off conflicting behavioral cues when in the patient's presence [p. 136]." Even though there is no medical evidence that cancer can be transmitted through human contact, many people act out of fear that it is contagious. Kleiman, Mantell, and Alexander (1977) suggest that this myth of contagion is pervasive among health-care providers and is a major cause of avoidance and rejection of the patient. Severo encountered physicians in major New York hospitals who admitted that they try to avoid shaking hands with cancer patients.

Several psychological factors seem to be involved in the antipathy to the sick. An explanation from a psychoanalytic perspective of the linkage between abnormality and wrongdoing has been proposed by Meng (reported in Barker et al., 1953). He finds that there are three primitive, often unconscious reactions to disease or injury: (1) the belief that physical disorders are a punishment for wrongdoing; (2) the belief that a disabled person has been unjustly punished and therefore is under pressure to do an evil act in order to balance the injustice; and (3) projection of one's own unacceptable desires upon the unfortunate other. All three reactions involve a perception of the afflicted person as dangerous.

Another factor mentioned by some writers is the great emphasis placed upon physical health and beauty as desirable attributes in this culture. Safilios-

Rothschild (1970) observes that the standards for physical integrity and perfection as well as for beauty appear to be very strict in Anglo-Saxon countries, especially among the middle classes, with any deviation from the highly admired state of perfection being punishable by social stigmatization. She writes, "Not only physical deformities or chronic invalidating illnesses, but also obesity (or even overweight), pimples, oily hair, 'bad' breath or sweating odors are considered intolerable and label the 'afflicted' individuals as deviants [p. 126]." The degree of aversion felt seems to be much greater in reaction to certain disabilities—such as skin disorders, amputation, body deformation, and cerebral palsy—than to deafness, blindness, or paralysis (Siller & Chipman, 1964). In this regard, Richardson, Hastorf, Goodman, and Dornbusch (1961) found that among all types of visible disabilities, facial disfigurements seemed to provoke the greatest amount of anxiety and aversion in children and adults. Those marked with facial anomalies provoke stronger aversion than do blind people, even though blindness is the most feared disability and the one considered to be most severe (Whiteman & Lukoff, 1965).

The role of cognitive–perceptual dispositions in the stigmatization process has also been discussed. Especially pertinent is Heider's (1944) notion of a fundamental tendency to see things of like quality as belonging together and as causally related. Thus negative states (such as sickness and deformity) are perceived as having negative causes (like wrongdoing on the part of the sufferer or someone else). Heider's concept of cognitive balance suggests that a person who displays a strongly negative attribute, such as a physical defect, will tend to be seen as having other negative attributes as well. Through this "spread" phenomenon of perceptual association, the nondisabled tend to create consistently negative impressions of the disabled individual, who is then viewed as inferior across a broad range of nonvisible characteristics simply on the basis of his visible or known disability. Thus, as shown in autobiographical essays written by the disabled (Hunt, 1966), the noninjured tend to talk down to a physically handicapped person as if he were mentally retarded and sometimes even as if he were deaf or blind, and they tend to be surprised at discovering that the disabled person may be quite intelligent and competent.

Prejudice may result from people's need to believe that the world is a just place where one gets what one deserves (Lerner, 1970). The possibility that someone can experience misfortune without in some way being responsible threatens this belief. Therefore, the hapless tend to be blamed for their plight. This not only protects the observer's belief in universal justice; it also provides a defense against the distressing thought that the same fate could befall him, regardless of how carefully he tried to prevent it from happening (Walster, 1966).

Experiments by Kleck and associates (Kleck, 1968; Kleck et al., 1966) have documented the conflicted nature of the majority's reactions to social contact with a crippled stranger. In face-to-face encounters with a confederate who either was or was not confined to a wheelchair, subjects evaluated the seemingly disabled person more favorably, made greater efforts to agree with his assumed opinions, and talked with him longer when they thought that by continuing the conversation they were helping the other person perform his job as an interviewer. However, subjects in the wheelchair condition, as compared with the normal condition, showed more motoric inhibition and were less willing to continue the interaction for its own sake.[6]

All of the foregoing suggests that attitudes toward persons with physical disorders tend to be ambivalent. On the friendly, compassionate side, there appears to be concern for those who suffer, respect for persons who cope with adversity, and acceptance of a norm of kindness toward the sick and injured; on the critical, rejectant side are apparent tendencies to dislike anyone who arouses fear or guilt and to perceive the handicapped as inferior, as perhaps responsible for their fate, as marginal people who should know their place and refrain from testing the limits of acceptance.

COMPARISON OF RACIAL AND DISABILITY ATTITUDES

Although my interest is in exploring the commonality of behavior toward blacks and disabled, there clearly are important differences in the stimulus properties of the two groups. The disability category is a much more heterogeneous one, embracing a host of functional and cosmetic defects of various kinds and degrees of severity. Hence there undoubtedly is more diversity in attitudes about people with physical disorders than in attitudes about a particular racial minority. Also, it seems likely that blacks, taken as a total group, experience more open hostility and rejection than do most individuals with bodily defects. The segregation, discrimination, and derogatory stereotyping that have long been imposed—and to a large extent continue to be imposed—upon members of this minority by the dominant group are both more inclusive and more extreme. Regarding favorable dispositions toward blacks and the disabled, social norms in this country probably grant the latter a larger measure of consideration.

There would also appear to be differences of a more qualitative nature in reactions to these marginal groups. For instance, even when whites feel compassion for black people who live in poverty they tend to blame them for not doing more to help themselves (Campbell, 1971). It is doubtful that a paraplegic, amputee, or blind person would similarly be expected to be self-sufficient. As

---

[6]Based on their own research on reactions to persons with physical or mental disabilities, Farina, Sherman, and Allen (1968) drew this conclusion: "Whether a stigma evokes favorable or unfavorable attitudes and behavior may be a complex matter involving at least the nature of the stigma, the characteristics of the perceiver, and the context of the interaction [p. 591]."

another example, although the nonstigmatized tend to avoid social contact with both blacks and the handicapped, the motives for avoidance are probably quite different. Anticipation of conflict over differing values, beliefs, and life-styles is probably a major consideration in avoiding racial minority members, whereas fear of not reacting appropriately to the other person's disability is probably more important in the case of the physically impaired.

Despite these and other important differences in attitudes and perceptions regarding the two groups, it seems worthwhile to investigate some of the ways in which they are reacted to similarly. The ambivalence assumption will be used as a principal basis for predicting certain kinds of behavioral commonality.

3 A Theory of Ambivalence-Induced Behavioral Amplification

I use the term *ambivalence* to denote a psychological condition in which a person has both positive (i.e., friendly, sympathetic, accepting) and negative (i.e., hostile, denigrative, rejecting) dispositions toward some group. The stronger the positive and negative dispositions and the more nearly equal their respective strengths, the greater the amount of ambivalence. Common observation suggests that ambivalence creates a tendency toward behavioral instability, in which extremely positive or negative responses may occur toward the object of ambivalence, depending on how the specific situation is structured. This phenomenon has been discussed by psychoanalytic writers. Thus Freud (1923/1961), who used the term *ambivalence* in reference to loving and hating the same person, believed that the conflict could be resolved by a "reactive displacement of cathexis," energy being withdrawn from one impulse and added to the other, opposite, impulse. He speculated that an instinct deriving from one particular source could transmit its energy to another instinct originating from a different source.

Guided by the psychoanalytic view of ambivalence, and making the assumption that attributes toward the mentally ill are essentially ambivalent, Gergen and Jones (1963) performed an experiment in which normal subjects displayed amplified positive or negative reactions to stimulus persons described as mental patients when the latter's behavior had had either favorable or unfavorable consequences for the subjects. The stimulus person's behavior presumably "split" the subject's ambivalent attitude so that one component was suppressed and the other component was enhanced. The ambivalence-amplification hypothesis that was tested in the Gergen and Jones experiment seems to be relevant to a large class of marginal groups, including blacks and the physically impaired.

It is conceivable that ambivalence toward blacks has had an amplification effect upon the white majority's reactions to their demands for equality during the past two decades. These reactions have been marked by wide swings between accommodation on the one hand, and strong resistance on the other. Consider, for example, the ground swell of popular support that made possible the civil rights legislation of the 1960s and the historically unprecedented antipoverty expenditures of the Johnson Administration. Consider also the recent move toward public and private retrenchment on many issues of equal opportunity for blacks. Of course, demographic, political, and economic developments play a fundamental role in the shaping of the dominant group's behavior toward nonwhite minorities. What is proposed here is that in addition to the macrolevel determination of this behavior, its seeming instability and polarity over relatively brief periods of time suggest the possibility of a psychological process of response amplification.

Response amplification might operate not only with respect to public policy formulation but also in social interactions. In a suggestive study by Dienstbier (1970), a questionnaire technique was used to compare the amount of verbal liking and acceptance shown by white subjects toward white and black stimulus persons who were supposed to have either socially desirable or socially undesirable beliefs and values. When favorable beliefs were ascribed to both stimulus persons, the black person received greater acceptance than the white person. But when unfavorable beliefs were ascribed to both, the opposite outcome occurred. Thus subjects made stronger responses, either positive or negative, to blacks than to whites, as a function of certain nonracial features of the situation.

Turning to the physically impaired, it is well known that they have traditionally received special types of consideration and help. When they have been unable to obtain needed care from their families, it has often been provided by the community, even if grudgingly. The modern period has seen the emergence of organized charity, government pensions, and free hospitals and clinics for the handicapped. (For example, see Scott's, 1969, description of the enormous network of publicly and privately supported agencies for the blind that exists in the United States.) However, historical instances of harsh maltreatment and rejection of the sick and injured are also too well known to require documentation. Just as the New Testament conception of Christ the Healer has encouraged compassionate behavior, other beliefs have led to cruelty and neglect. But as yet there have been only a few studies specifically designed to test the hypothesis that behavior toward physically handicapped individuals can be either more positive or more negative than comparable behavior toward normals.

A FRAMEWORK FOR STUDYING
AMBIVALENCE EFFECTS[1]

Psychoanalytic theory calls attention to the phenomenon of ambivalence-induced behavioral amplification, but it fails to specify either the psychological mediators of this relationship or the conditions under which it is likely to occur. This author believes that ambivalence creates in the person a high vulnerability to emotional tension in situations of contact with the attitudinal object or cues associated with the attitudinal object. Specifically with respect to a stigmatized stimulus person, an actor may perceive himself (consciously or unconsciously) as having friendly feelings for a more-or-less discredited, unworthy other, or as having aversive feelings about someone less fortunate than himself. Either type of self-referent cognition should pose a threat to the actor's self-image as one who is humane yet judicious in his evaluations and treatment of others. It is also proposed that this sense of threat gives rise to threat-reductive efforts that are often manifested as extreme behavior toward the attitudinal object, either positive or negative depending on the structure of the situation.

Further, in a given contact situation, initially occurring stimulus events might accord with one component of an ambivalent disposition but contradict the other, opposite, component. (For example, the actor might unintentionally help or harm the other person, or the latter might reveal favorable or unfavorable traits.) Such stimulus events should tend to increase the salience of the attitudinal conflict, hence the threat to self-regard, resulting in heightened efforts at threat reduction. These efforts could take the form of either defense or denial of the discredited attitude. (For example, the actor might reinterpret the stimulus events so that they no longer contradicted the attitude, or he might engage in overt actions that compensated for the attitude.) Which of the alternative means of threat reduction was used in a particular instance would largely be determined by relative cost and availability and (as mentioned previously) would often be observable as response amplification—i.e., as behavior toward the stigmatized person that was more extreme than behavior toward a nonstigmatized but otherwise similar person in the same type of situation.

What is being suggested is a threefold dichotomization of interaction situations involving a nonstigmatized actor–subject and a stigmatized other, in which ambivalence-amplification effects will occur: (1) the process would begin with an input of relevant information to the actor from *self* or *other;* (2) the input would discredit either the *positive* or *negative* component of an ambivalent disposition; and (3) the prepotent coping strategy would be either to *defend* or *deny* the discredited attitude. The various situations are outlined in Table 3.1 and discussed in the following paragraphs.

1. *Positive input from actor.*   The subject is induced initially to evaluate the other favorably or to help the other in some way. If the act is experienced as freely chosen, the subject will tend to perceive it as inconsistent with his negative attitude about the stigmatized group. He may feel that he has overrated the person due to inattention, carelessness, or a lapse in judgment—or that he has favored the other for irrelevant reasons. These cognitions may pose a threat to his self-image as a judicious, fair-minded person. Perhaps the usual coping strategy in

---

[1]An earlier statement of this theory can be found in Katz and Glass (1979).

TABLE 3.1
A Three-Factor Model of Interaction Situations
Involving a Nonstigmatized Actor and a Stigmatized Other

Behavior and Attitudes[a]	Positive Initial Input		Negative Initial Input	
	Self as Source	Other as Source	Self as Source	Other as Source
Examples of initial behavior	Actor helps, praises Other	Other helps Actor, displays positive traits	Actor harms, denigrates Other	Other harms Actor, displays negative traits
Nature of discredited attitude	Critical, aversive	Critical, aversive	Friendly, sympathetic	Friendly, sympathetic
Examples of behavior defending discredited attitude	Actor rejects, denigrates Other	Actor rejects, denigrates Other	Actor helps, praises Other	Actor helps, praises Other
Examples of behavior denying discredited attitude	Actor helps, praises Other	Actor helps, praises Other	Actor rejects, deingrates Other	Actor rejects, denigrates Other

[a] Whether defense or denial of the discredited attitude will occur is determined by the relative cost and availability of these alternative means of threat reduction.

this type of situation is to deny the attitudinal component that is inconsistent with the behavior just enacted; that is, the subject reacts by expressing strong liking for the other person. This response would accord with the general hypothesis, derivable from dissonance theory (e.g., Schopler & Compere, 1971) and Bem's (1967) self-observation notion, that freely choosing to treat another kindly tends to increase the other's attractiveness. However, certain kinds of initially favorable behavior toward the stigmatized person might have an opposite (i.e., negative) effect on subsequent responses. Thus, if a subject was induced to over-reward a stigmatized person's task performance, under circumstances that made the act difficult to justify by raising the evaluation of the other person, the subject might resort to compensatory under-rewarding and denigration of the other on subsequent trials, thereby defending his negative attitude about the other's group.

2. *Positive input from other.* The stigmatized stimulus person displays socially desirable characteristics or engages in behavior that is beneficial to the actor. Thus the input is consistent with the subject's positive attitude about the stigmatized group but contradicts his negative attitude, thereby posing a threat to his self-image as an unprejudiced person. Threat-reductive behavior will likely take the form of denying prejudice by engaging in compensatory overvaluation of the stimulus person. Thus the subject may express amplified acceptance of the other on evaluative rating scales (Dienstbier, 1970) or exaggerated willingness to do the other person a small favor. However, if the initial stimulus input is somewhat ambiguous and opportunities for low-cost positive response are not readily available, the subject may reinterpret the input. A friendly gesture on the part of the other person may now be seen as an attempt at ingratiation (Jones, 1964) or at reducing the subject's freedom of choice (Brehm, 1966). The actor may then display strong rejection of the other person.

3. *Negative input from actor.* The subject is induced initially to insult or physically hurt the other person. If the subject believes his action was freely chosen, he will tend to perceive it as inconsistent with his positive attitude about the stigmatized group, and thereby experience a threat to his self-image as a humane, unprejudiced person. Previous research with nonstigmatized subjects and stimulus persons indicates that unintentional harm-doers often behave afterward as though they were trying to reduce feelings of guilt. Denigration of the victim may occur (presumably as a means of justifying the injurious act), or compensatory helping of the victim may occur. Relative opportunity largely determines which means of guilt reduction is adopted by the harm-doer (cf. review by Walster, Berscheid, & Walster, 1970). In the present situation, a harm-doer who denigrated a stigmatized victim on a post–harm-doing rating scale would, in effect, be denying his positive attitude by asserting that the victim (and by implication the victim's group) deserved to be treated harshly. But the outcome would probably be different if instead of being required to evaluate the person he had just injured, the subject was requested by the victim to provide some needed assistance at a task. The subject would now have an opportunity to demonstrate sympathy for the stigmatized other by complying with the request

for help. In this way, the subject could restore his self-image as one who has compassion for the underdog.

4. *Negative input from other.* The stimulus person displays socially undesirable characteristics or behaves in a way that is detrimental to the subject. This input is consistent with the subject's negative attitude about the stigmatized group, but it contradicts his positive attitude, thereby posing a threat to his self-image as a discerning person who has sympathy only for those who deserve it. The usual coping strategy in this type of situation is probably to deny the friendly attitude by engaging in very negative behavior against the stimulus person, such as extreme denigration (Dienstbier, 1970). However, if the initial stimulus events are somewhat ambiguous and there exist ordinary situational constraints against expressing hostility, the subject may choose to reinterpret the stimulus events. Thus, on a cooperative task where a stigmatized partner's errors have caused the subject to lose money, the subject may attribute the other's poor performance to inexperience rather than lack of effort and hence react with friendly encouragement and assistance.

Comparison of Model With Other Inconsistency Theories

The notion of ambivalence-induced amplification of responses can be related to theories of attitude change that postulate a tendency for inconsistent cognitive structures to move toward a state of consistency (e.g., Abelson & Rosenberg, 1958; Heider, 1958; Osgood & Tannenbaum, 1955). However, these theories tend to be less concerned with affective than with cognitive inconsistency and have not dealt specifically with the phenomenon of ambivalence, i.e., of inconsistent dispositions toward a single attitudinal object.

More relevant to the present formulation is Rokeach's (1973) value–attitude consistency theory. Rokeach proposes that inconsistencies between values and attitudes which implicate the self-concept tend to generate self-dissatisfaction, which in turn gives rise to cognitive and behavioral change. In an experimental test of the theory, Rokeach confronted white subjects with discrepancies between their general values (specifically, their preferential rankings of the values *freedom* and *equality*) and their civil rights attitudes. Subjects reported feelings of self-dissatisfaction and showed long-term favorable changes in attitudes and behavior toward blacks. Thus both Rokeach's and this writer's theories deal with the behavioral effects of inconsistent cognitions relating to an object group (such as blacks) when the inconsistency threatens positive self-regard. However, one important difference between the theories is that Rokeach's does not employ the notion of response amplification—i.e., of extremely positive or *extremely negative* behavior occurring as a consequence of value–attitude inconsistency.

The ambivalence model also has points of similarity to Festinger's theory of cognitive dissonance—particularly to Aronson's (1969) modified version of this theory, according to which strong dissonance occurs only when the self-concept is centrally involved. But the ambivalence model goes beyond dissonance theory in proposing that more psychic conflict will be aroused when a new perception (e.g., of one's own behavior) contradicts *a component of an ambivalent disposition* than will be aroused when it contradicts *a simple univalent attitude*. For example, the ambivalence formulation states that unintentional harming of another will be more distressing to a harm-doer who has both friendly and hostile feelings toward the victim than to a harm-doer in whom friendliness is clearly the dominant sentiment. The notion that ambivalence will heighten the intensity of dissonance effects is not incompatible with dissonance theory (as modified by Aronson), but it is not implied in the theory in any obvious sense.

Research Implications of the Model

The four types of stimulus-input situations that were described earlier suggest a number of experimental paradigms for the testing of predictions. The next two chapters deal with studies of the effects of unintentional harm-doing on subsequent behavior toward black or physically handicapped victims. Presented in Chapter 4 are experiments that examine the amplification hypothesis as applied to post–harm-doing denigration of victims. Chapter 5 is concerned with experiments in which harm-doers are afforded an opportunity to do a favor for the injured person. Later chapters describe tests of other implications of the model, usually involving studies of both black and disabled stimulus persons.

4 The Scapegoating of Stigmatized Victims

Of the various social interaction situations depicted in the previous chapter in Table 3.1, the first to be investigated was that in which a nonstigmatized actor is initially induced to harm a stigmatized other and then is provided an opportunity to denigrate him. That harm-doers will often denigrate their victims has been demonstrated in several experiments that did not employ a stigma variable (cf. review by Berscheid & Walster, 1969). Such denigration has been interpreted as a way of reducing the moral discomfort that results from hurting another (called "guilt" by Freedman, 1970; "distress over inequity" by Walster, Berscheid, & Walster, 1970; and "dissonance" by Davidson, 1964; Davis & Jones, 1960; Glass, 1964). The common assumption is that denigration functions to justify the harmful act by lowering the worth of the injured person and that the greater the discomfort of the harm-doer, the stronger the tendency to denigrate.

In the experimental paradigms that have been used to study the denigration of victims, the subject is always given a nonaggressive rationale for inflicting harm (e.g., he is asked to take the role of "instructor in an investigation of human learning" and to give electric shocks to a "learner" as punishment for errors). The moral tension or discomfort experienced by the subject can therefore be said to be associated with harm-doing that was unintentional. In this type of situation, having an ambivalent attitude toward the other person should tend to heighten the arousal of tension after having injured him. That is, conflicted feelings of sympathy and disdain for the other should cause the subject to question his motives for delivering the painful stimuli—to suspect that he may have enjoyed hurting the other person and perhaps had even inflicted more punishment than was necessary. Hence the subject should feel more culpable than he would if his initial attitude was one of simple hostility, friendliness, or neutrality; and the tendency to denigrate should be stronger.

If the initial attitude was simply hostile, the other person would be perceived from the start as deserving harm, and there would be no strong need to justify the harm-doing through further derogation. If the initial attitude was simply friendly, the subject would feel compassion for the victim and perhaps some guilt, but less guilt than if he had reason to suspect himself of gratifying a hostile impulse at the other's expense. Finally, if the initial attitude was neutral or indifferent, there would be relatively little concern over the victim's plight and relatively little reason to question one's motives for obeying the experimenter's instructions.

To test this line of reasoning, experiments were done in which white normal subjects gave impression ratings of black or physically handicapped persons immediately before and after being induced to hurt them. Sometimes measures of attitude toward the respective stigma groups were taken at a separate session. The aim was to show that: (1) decrements in evaluation were larger after harming a stigmatized than a nonstigmatized person; and (2) variations among subjects in the tendency to denigrate stigmatized victims were a function of individual differences in attitudinal ambivalence.

EXPERIMENT ON DENIGRATION
OF A BLACK VICTIM

Method

In this study by Katz, Glass, and Cohen (1973), the subjects were white male students at a college in New York City and were paid for participating. When the subject arrived at the laboratory waiting room, a black or white male confederate, posing as a fellow subject, was already there. A few minutes later the experimenter, a white male graduate student, arrived to escort the men to the laboratory, where they were shown to chairs. The experimenter explained that the study dealt with extrasensory perception, including how people's first impressions of one another influenced their ability to communicate through ESP.

The men were given a 20-item impression-rating questionnaire consisting of five trait clusters—likeability, warmth, conceit, intelligence, adjustment—each made up of four brief statements, two worded positively and two negatively. Ratings were made on a 6-point scale reflecting degree of agreement–disagreement with each statement.[1] Next, subjects received either the Mild Shock or Strong Shock instructions. The shocks ostensibly were to be administered by one person (the message sender) to the other (the receiver) as punishment for errors. Each man was given a "sample shock," which for the true subject was either very weak or painfully strong, depending on the condition.

---

[1] An obtained Kuder–Richardson reliability coefficient of .87 for the before-shock ratings was in close agreement with the .90 value reported by Davis and Jones.

Then lots were drawn to determine the assignment of task roles, and (by pre-arrangement) the confederate always got the receiver role. The experimenter seated him at a table, and electrodes were attached to his hand. The subject was placed at an adjacent table on the other side of a partition. In front of him was a metal box labeled "Shock Generator." He was shown how to use a switch labeled either "Slight Shock—30V" or "Strong Shock—135 V."

A procedure was explained whereby the subject was to concentrate on mentally transmitting one of two color stimuli to the partner, who was then to signal his response by pressing one of two buttons wired to colored lights on the subject's side of the partition. Twenty trials were run, on 10 of which the confederate made "errors" and was supposed to be shocked by the subject. Next, the confederate was sent to another room, and the impression rating scale was again administered to the subject, followed by a postexperimental questionnaire and a debriefing.

The design of the experiment, then, was a 2×2 factorial as follows: Strong Shock/Black Confederate, Mild Shock/Black Confederate, Strong Shock/White Confederate, and Mild Shock/White Confederate. Ten subjects were randomly assigned to each condition.

Results

Subjects' ratings of the painfulness of the sample shocks they received and their impressions of the painfulness of the shocks delivered to the confederate provided a check on the adequacy of the manipulation of shock level. Both estimates were substantially higher in the Strong Shock condition than in the Mild Shock condition ($ps < .001$), suggesting that the manipulation was adequate.

The major dependent variable was the change in subjects' evaluations of the confederate's personality. The mean change scores along with the mean evaluations prior to the administration of shock are presented for each experimental condition in Table 4.1. It can be seen that the four experimental groups did not

TABLE 4.1
Mean Before and Change Scores for Evaluation of Black
and White Confederates Receiving Two Levels of Shock

| | Experimental Condition | | | |
| | Black Confederate | | White Confederate | |
	Strong Shock	Mild Shock	Strong Shock	Mild Shock
Before scores	19.2	14.3	16.3	15.4
Change scores	−11.9	7.2	0.0	−0.8

Note: The higher the score, the more favorable the rating. $N = 10$ in all cells.

differ significantly in their initial ratings of the confederate. But after administering shock, subjects in the Strong Shock condition changed their evaluations less favorably than did subjects in the Mild Shock condition. F (1,36) = 4.66, p < .05—an effect due entirely to the change scores of subjects in the Black Confederate condition; F (1,36) = 5.28, p < .05 for the Race × Shock interaction. Strong Shock/Black Confederate was the only treatment in which the postshock ratings were less favorable than the preshock ones. An analysis of covariance of post scores, in which prescores were the covariate, yielded similar results. Thus the experimental prediction was upheld.

One of the main assumptions underlying the prediction was that subjects in the Strong Shock/Black Confederate condition would feel more culpable after delivering the shock than subjects in any other condition. Data from an item in the postexperimental questionnaire were relevant to this assumption. The item dealt with how much guilt the subjects experienced after giving the shock to the confederate. Self-ratings of guilt were higher in the Strong Shock condition than in the Mild Shock condition, F (1,36) = 22.95, p < .001. There were no significant correlations within any shock–race treatments between guilt ratings and derogation. The apparent lack of association in the Strong Shock/Black Confederate treatment may have been due to a ceiling artifact in the guilt ratings. Most of the ratings in this treatment were clustered at the high end of the 7-point scale (M = 6.0).

An additional finding was that Strong Shock subjects, as compared with Mild Shock subjects, believed that the confederate had suffered greater physical injury, F (1,36) = 20.25, p < .001. There were also three trends in which Strong Shock subjects appeared to believe more strongly that the experiment was a worthwhile and important experience, F (1,36) = 2.88, p < .10; that the experimenter was intelligent, F (1,36) = 3.49, p < .10; and that he was reliable, F (1,36) = 4.07, p < .10. These nonsignificant differences suggest that Strong Shock subjects may have sought to reduce guilt by magnifying the value of the experiment and the competence of the experimenter.

EFFECT OF ATTITUDE ON DENIGRATION
OF A BLACK VICTIM

Method

To study the relationship between ambivalence and denigration, Katz et al. (1973) used a procedure that was an exact replication of the Strong Shock/Black Confederate condition of the first experiment. In addition, the subjects (22 New York City white male college students) filled out a racial attitude questionnaire at a separate session, ostensibly as part of a different project. The attitude questionnaire contained two kinds of items, prejudice and sympathy. Prejudice was

TABLE 4.2
Mean Before and Change Scores for Evaluation
of Black Confederate by Four Types of Subjects

	Attitudinal Type			
	High Prej.— High Symp. (N = 7)	High Prej.— Low Symp. (N = 5)	Low Prej.— High Symp. (N = 5)	Low Prej.— Low Symp. (N = 5)
Before scores	4.1	1.2	17.8	11.4
Change scores	−4.3	15.8	6.2	5.0

measured by 30 items from Woodmansee and Cook's (1967) Racial Attitude Inventory. The measure of sympathy was an adaptation of Schuman and Harding's (1963) scale on sympathetic identification with the underdog. Each of its 13 items asks the respondent to indicate how he thinks a black person would react to a particular instance of prejudice or discrimination.[2] Subjects' scores on each scale were split at the median as evenly as possible, resulting in four categories representing the various combinations of high versus low prejudice and high versus low sympathy.

Results

As in the first study, the major dependent variable was the change in evaluations of the confederate. The mean change scores and preshock evaluations for each experimental condition are presented in Table 4.2. Before giving shocks to the confederate, High Prejudice subjects tended to give somewhat less favorable evaluations than did Low Prejudice subjects, $F (1,18) = 3.09$, $p < .10$. Afterward, High Sympathy subjects showed significantly less favorable change than Low Sympathy subjects, $F (1,18) = 6.87$, $p < .05$. However, this difference was due entirely to the ratings of subjects in the High Prejudice group; $F (1,18) = 7.22$, $p < .05$ for the Prejudice × Sympathy interaction. An analysis of covariance of post scores, in which prescores were the covariate, yielded similar results. Thus the experimental prediction was upheld.

It may be noted that both the pre and change ratings in Table 4.2 are quite different from the ratings obtained in the Strong Shock/Black Confederate condition of the earlier experiment (shown in Table 4.1). A possible explanation is that the two studies used different experimenters and black confederates, and recruited subjects from different colleges.

---

[2]To estimate the reliability of the prejudice and sympathy items for the present population, the questionnaire was administered to a total of 90 students at the same college as the experimental subjects. Reliability, as measured by Cronbach's coefficient alpha, was .69 for prejudice and .65 for sympathy, and the product moment correlation between prejudice and sympathy was −.20. These

EXPERIMENT ON DENIGRATION
OF A HANDICAPPED VICTIM

Method

This study by Katz, Glass, Lucido, and Farber (1977) was similar to the two experiments just described except that it employed a different type of stigma, physical disability. The subjects were 60 New York City women, between the ages of 18 and 45, randomly drawn from a pool of paid volunteers who had filled out a psychological test battery several weeks earlier. Included in the battery was a modified version of Kaplan's (1972) split semantic differential scales for assessing attitudinal ambivalence. The target group was *the physically handicapped*. This instrument consisted of 16 unipolar, 6-point (0–5) evaluative scales, of which 8 had positive trait labels (e.g., "warm") and 8 had polar opposite labels (e.g., "cold"). An introductory statement explained that one purpose of the scales was to permit people to express duality of feeling when it existed.[3]

When the subject arrived at the laboratory waiting room, a 22-year-old white female confederate, posing as a fellow subject, was already there. For half the subjects she was seated in a wheelchair; for the other half she was seated in an ordinary chair.[4] The same confederate was used for the entire experiment. The experimenter was a male graduate student. The rest of the experimental procedure was virtually identical with that of the first racial experiment, except that noise signals instead of electric shocks were ostensibly administered by subjects to the confederate (who wore earphones) as feedback for "errors" on the ESP task. To half the subjects, the signal was described as "a loud and annoying burst of high frequency sound waves . . . a punishing noise . . . painful . . . but not so intense as to cause permanent damage to the ear." To the other half of the sample, the sound signal was described as a mild tone.

---

reliability coefficients were somewhat lower than those obtained by Woodmansee and Cook, but the correlation between prejudice and sympathy was highly similar to theirs, indicating that these attitudes were relatively independent of each other.

[3]Kaplan's ambivalence score is defined as total affect minus unambivalent affect, where total affect is the sum of the positive scale ratings plus the sum of the negative scale ratings, and unambivalent affect is the difference between the sums of the positive and negative ratings, disregarding sign. The reliabilities of the positive and negative scale components, as estimated by Cronbach's Coefficient Alpha, were .89 and .87, respectively.

[4]In all of the studies that my co-workers and I conducted with physically handicapped confederates, disability was indicated by confinement to a wheelchair. This device was used because it is a convenient way of indicating major physical dysfunction. The wheelchair is an internationally recognized symbol of disability, thereby reflecting a common understanding of the basic functional limitations of people who use wheelchairs. Moreover, in studies that asked nondisabled subjects to state their relative liking for people with various types of physical disorder, those depicted in wheelchairs tended to be ranked in the middle (e.g., Alessi & Anthony, 1969; Richardson & Emerson, 1970; Shears & Jensema, 1969). This suggests that reactions to a wheelchair-defined disability may be taken as reasonably representative of reactions to a range of physical disorders.

Results

Subjects' ratings of the painfulness of the sound stimuli they delivered to the confederate were considerably higher in the Loud Noise condition than in the Mild Noise one, F (1,56) = 35.88, $p < .001$. This suggests that the noise-level manipulation was adequate.

Evaluation of the Confederate.   Prior to the ESP trial series, Noxious Noise subjects were significantly less favorable in their evaluations of the confederate than Mild Noise subjects, F (1,56) = 4.69, $p < .05$. Inasmuch as the confederate did not know at this stage in the procedure which noise condition was to be run, hence could not have unconsciously biased the results, this difference in Before ratings would seem to be due to random error. There was also a slight tendency for Before ratings to be more favorable in the Wheelchair condition than in the Nonwheelchair condition, F (1,56) = 2.56, $p < .15$.

To test the prediction that evaluations of the confederate would be most detrimentally affected in the Noxious Noise/Wheelchair group, a 2 × 2 analysis of covariance was done on the After scores, using the Before scores as the covariate. A significant interaction was obtained: F (1,56) = 4.78, $p < .05$. In Table 4.3 are presented the Before score means, the mean differences between Before scores and unadjusted After scores, and the adjusted means for the After scores. As anticipated, the adjusted After scores show that the greatest amount of denigration occurred in the Noxious Noise/Wheelchair cell. The difference scores reveal a similar pattern. There was also a marginally significant main effect of noise level on the After scores, F (1,56) = 3.54, $p < .10$, with Noxious Noise subjects rating the confederate less favorably than did Mild Noise subjects.

Ambivalence and Denigration.   As mentioned earlier, ambivalence about physically handicapped people in general (Kaplan scale) was indexed as the sum

TABLE 4.3
Means for Before Scores, Before–After Change Scores, and
Adjusted After Scores for Evaluations of the Confederate

| | *Experimental Condition* | | | |
| | *Wheelchair* | | *Normal* | |
	Noxious Noise	*Mild Noise*	*Noxious Noise*	*Mild Noise*
Before scores	30.8	37.5	26.9	32.2
Change scores	−11.5	−0.1	−3.3	−3.4
Adjusted After scores	20.7	31.3	29.1	28.4

Note: N = 15 in all cells.

of one's ratings of favorable and unfavorable traits, minus the absolute difference between the ratings of favorable and unfavorable traits. Favorableness and unfavorableness scores were converted to standard scores before deriving ambivalence. To assess the relationship between ambivalence and denigration of the confederate in the Loud Noise/Wheelchair condition, Pearson correlations were computed in that condition between ambivalence scores and Before evaluations of the confederate, and between ambivalence scores and Before–After change scores. For the former, r (13) = .08, $p > .20$; for the latter, r (13) = .42, $p < .12$. Thus the predicted relationship was not significant. To see whether the relationship would be stronger if only subjects with extreme ambivalence scores were considered, those in the highest and lowest ambivalence tertiles in the Noxious Noise/Wheelchair condition were compared on Before evaluations of the confederate and on Before–After change scores ($N = 5$ for each tertile subgroup). The Before scores were similar for the two subgroups, t (9) < 1.00; but the change scores of the high-ambivalence subjects were more negative ($M = 24.6$) than those of the low-ambivalence subjects ($M = 6.0$), t (9) = 2.00, $p = .08$, indicating a trend in the predicted direction.

Correlations between ambivalence scores and Before–After change scores were also done in each of the other experimental conditions; as expected, they were all very low. Next, scores on the positive and negative trait scales were separately correlated with Before–After change scores in the Noxious Noise/ Wheelchair condition. The respective rs were close to zero; that is, neither favorable nor unfavorable feelings about the handicapped, considered separately, were predictive of harm-doers' reactions to the confederate.

Self-Ratings of Guilt.   On the postexperimental questionnaire, subjects were asked to rate how uneasy they felt and how much guilt they experienced over delivering the noise stimuli. Noxious Noise subjects rated themselves higher on both items ($ps < .001$), but neither the guilt nor the uneasiness scores correlated with evaluations of the confederate within any of the conditions.

DISCUSSION

It was found that harm-doers were more likely to derogate a black or disabled victim than a white normal one and that the tendency to scapegoat the stigmatized person was related to individual differences in ambivalence toward the minority group as a whole (though the relationship was not a strong one in the case of the handicapped victim). That guilt over harm-doing was a factor mediating between ambivalence and scapegoating is not supported by the results. Although in these studies subjects' self-reports of guilt were higher in the Strong Shock and Noxious Noise conditions than in the Mild Shock and Mild Noise conditions, they were not significantly higher when the victim was black or handicapped as compared with white, nonhandicapped. Nor were the self-reports of guilt correlated with amount of scapegoating within the experimental condition where pain was inflicted on a minority person. However, the obtained guilt scores do not necessarily reflect subjects' actual levels of guilt arousal immediately after delivering the noxious stimuli. Not only was there an opportunity to reduce guilt through derogation before the self-ratings of guilt were obtained, but verbal denial of guilt may also have been used by subjects as a guilt-reductive mechanism.

Nonetheless, one may ask whether it is really necessary to employ a concept of guilt, or threat to self-regard, in order to account for the present results. Does not Lerner's (1970) just-world hypothesis account for the data just as well? If one were dealing only with the interaction effect of stigma and harm-doing, it could perhaps be argued that Lerner's postulated need to believe that people in this world get what they deserve and deserve what they get provides an adequate explanation. It would only be necessary to assume that subjects were predisposed to perceive blacks and the handicapped as more deserving of misfortune than nonhandicapped whites.[5] But the just-world hypothesis cannot readily account for the obtained relationship between individual differences in ambivalence and amount of scapegoating of minority victims. Surely the predisposition to perceive blacks and the handicapped as deserving victims should have been strongest in subjects who were unambiguously prejudiced against these groups.[6] Moreover, a study by Regan (1971) suggests that guilt is a more important determinant of behavior toward people one has harmed than is the need to believe in a just world (whereas the latter apparently is a more important determinant of behavior on the part of those who have merely observed the harm-doing).

Assuming that subjects used derogation of the black or handicapped confederate to justify their harm-doing and thereby reduce their guilt, a question arises as to why derogation was preferred over various alternative modes of guilt reduction, such as denial of responsibility, maximization of the positive aspects of the harmful action (e.g., by emphasizing the importance of the experiment), or minimization of the victim's suffering. A plausible answer is that requiring

---

[5]Actually, there was virtually no evidence of denigration when the victim was nonstigmatized (Tables 4.1 and 4.3). In the earlier, nonstigma, studies employing the teacher–learner paradigm (e.g., Davis & Jones, 1960; Glass, 1964), the attempt had been to heighten the arousal of guilt or dissonance over the harm-doing by informing subjects at the outset that they were free to withdraw from the experiment if they did not wish to deliver the shocks. But since our aim was to highlight a stigma effect, we tried to minimize the amount of internal conflict associated with the harm-doing per se by assigning subjects to the teacher role with no option to refuse.

[6]I am assuming, of course, that our measures of prejudice and sympathy were valid and that the ambivalence measure did not reflect an unwillingness to admit the true extent of one's negative feelings.

subjects to do a second evaluation of the confederate immediately after the shock or noise series made derogation a highly available mode of guilt reduction.[7] The next chapter deals with experiments in which harm-doers were provided an opportunity to do a favor for the victim, instead of an opportunity to denigrate that person.

---

[7]Using the teacher-learner paradigm but different response measures, Brock and Buss (1962) found that subjects reduced their estimates of the painfulness of the shocks they had administered, and Buss and Brock (1963) observed that harm-doers repressed information about the harmfulness of the shocks. In a related investigation by Brock and Buss (1964), self-ratings of guilt were lower when subjects had an opportunity to communicate with their victim afterward.

5 Helping Stigmatized Victims

The research to be presented now examines the favorable side of the response-amplification hypothesis about the behavioral consequences of unintentionally injuring another person. The attempt will be to show that when actors have a chance to do a favor for someone they have just hurt, instead of being required to evaluate him (as in the studies described in Chapter 4), they will give more aid to a stigmatized victim than to one who is not stigmatized. This expectation follows from the same line of reasoning as did the earlier denigration prediction, inasmuch as helping and denigration are assumed to be functionally equivalent behaviors in the post–harm-doing situation—i.e., alternative means of reducing moral discomfort.[1]

That transgressors are likely to engage in compensatory helping of their victims when afforded an opportunity to do so has been demonstrated in experiments that employed nondisabled white stimulus persons (Berscheid and Walster, 1967; Carlsmith and Gross, 1969; Freedman, Wallington, and Bless, 1967; and others). According to the ambivalence-amplification model, this helping tendency should be especially strong when the injured person is black or disabled. Three experiments were conducted to test this proposition.

EXPERIMENT ON HELPING A BLACK VICTIM

Method

Subjects in this study by Katz, Glass, Lucido, and Farber (1979) were white male college students in New York City, who volunteered for pay and were tested individually. They were induced by a white male experimenter to make either

---

[1]Recently, Kenrick, Reich, and Cialdini (1976) have tried to show that denigration of a victim does not tend to reduce later compensatory helping efforts; however, their demonstration was faulted by the use of a compensatory response that entailed neither psychological nor material cost to the subject.

highly insulting, critical remarks (High Criticism condition) or neutral remarks (Low Criticism condition) to a black or white male confederate posing as a fellow subject. The cover story for this harm-doing manipulation was that people's emotional reactions to criticism from a stranger were being investigated. This fact, it was stated, had to be concealed for a while from the "other subject," who had randomly been assigned to the target role. After making their fictitious evaluative comments to the confederate, men in the High Criticism condition were led to believe that their harsh words had upset the other person, who, unfortunately, had had to leave to get to a part-time job, before the experimenter could fully convince him of the bogus nature of the criticism. Those in the Low Criticism condition were merely told that the partner had had to leave to get to a job. There were approximately 25 subjects in each of the four Race × Criticism conditions.

In all conditions the subject at this point thought that the experiment was over. He was sent to an office where he was paid and signed out by a white female secretary, who then handed him a note supposedly left for him by the confederate. The note stated that the confederate was doing an independent research project for a psychology course and needed "one more subject to finish up the sample." The project was described as dealing with the effects of repetition of a simple motor task on uniformity of response. The subject was requested to write a brief specimen sentence as many times as possible in a booklet attached to the note, and then to leave the booklet with the secretary, to be picked up by the confederate at another time. The number of times the subject wrote the specimen sentence constituted the measure of helping behavior. Afterward he was met by the experimenter, asked to fill out a short questionnaire, and debriefed.

Two completely different experimental teams were used, each consisting of experimenter, white confederate, black confederate, and secretary. The respective teams ran the same number of subjects in each experimental condition. Hence the design was a 2 × 2 × 2 factorial (Race × Level of Criticism × Experimenters).

Results

Subjects were asked in the postexperimental questionnaire how they thought their comments about the partner had affected him. Responding on a 7-point scale ranging from very positive to very negative, the ratings of the High Criticism group were substantially more negative than those of the Low Criticism group ($p < .001$ for the main effect). Thus the manipulation of harm-doing appears to have been adequate.

Helping Behavior. Analysis of variance of the helping scores showed a significant main effect of race: More sentences were written for the black confederates ($M = 27.08$) than for the white ones ($M = 21.60$), $F (1,91) = 3.86$, $p < .05$. Also, the Race × Criticism interaction (shown in Table 5.1) was signifi-

TABLE 5.1
Mean Number of Sentences Written for Black and
White Partners in High and Low Criticism Conditions

	Race of Confederate	
Level of Criticism	Black	White
High	36.10 (25)	12.20 (25)
Low	18.06 (25)	20.45 (24)

Note: Cell Ns are in parentheses.

cant, $F (1,91) = 5.77$, $p < .02$. Low Criticism subjects gave slightly more help to white than to black confederates, $t (91) < 1$, whereas in the High Criticism condition, the black confederates received much more help than the white ones, $t (91) = 4.44$, $p < .001$. Looking at criticism effects within race, High Criticism led to a significant increase in amount of aid given black partners, $t (91) = 3.35$, $p < .01$, but produced a relatively small, nonsignificant decrease in amount of help given the whites, $t (91) = 1.53$, $p < .15$. The results on helping clearly support the amplification prediction.

Other Findings.   The guilt ratings (7-point scale) of High Criticism subjects were significantly higher ($M = 2.95$) than those of Low Criticism subjects ($M = 1.60$), $F (1,91) = 18.52$, $p < .001$. There was also a trend toward higher guilt ratings when the confederate was black ($M = 2.60$) than when he was white ($M = 2.04$), $F = 3.52$, $p < .06$. Further, although the expected interaction of race and criticism was not significant ($p = .18$), it can be seen in Table 5.2 that self-reports of guilt were higher in Black/High Criticism than in White/High Criticism, $t (91) = 2.37$, $p < .02$, whereas in the two Low Criticism cells, guilt scores were about the same. Thus there was some support for the assumption that harming a black partner would be more guilt-arousing than harming a white partner. However, guilt and helping were not related to one another in the High Criticism cells.

TABLE 5.2
Mean Guilt Ratings in
the Four Race/Criticism Conditions

	Race of Confederate	
Level of Criticism	Black	White
High	3.43 (25)	2.48 (24)
Low	1.77 (25)	1.61 (24)

Note: Cell Ns are in parentheses.

FIRST EXPERIMENT ON HELPING
A HANDICAPPED VICTIM

Method

This was a further investigation of the compensatory-helping hypothesis, using a physically handicapped person instead of a black person as the victim of harm-doing. The subjects were 82 white, nonhandicapped females who were recruited through an ad in a New York City newspaper and paid for participating. Their ages ranged from 17 to 65, with a mean of 30.1. The procedure for inducing unintentional harm-doing was the same as in the study of denigration of a disabled victim (Katz et al., 1977), which was described in Chapter 4. That is, subjects (tested individually) were persuaded to deliver noxiously loud or mild sound signals to a confederate, as feedback for errors on an ESP task. In the present experiment, the confederate was a young woman who told the subject she was a college student. Half the time she was in a wheelchair, and half the time she appeared to be physically normal. Following the ESP trial series, the procedure for measuring willingness to help the confederate was much the same as in the experiment just described on helping of a black victim. That is, the confederate was sent to another room, supposedly to fill out a questionnaire; a short while later, the subject was informed fictitiously that the confederate had been allowed to leave by an assistant who was unaware that the experimenter wanted to see her again. The subject was left with the assistant to be signed out and paid; then the assistant handed the subject the note from the confederate asking her to participate in the study of handwriting repetition, etc. The design, then, was a 2 × 2 factorial (Noxious or Mild Noise × Disabled or Nondisabled Confederate).

Results

Subjects in the Noxious Noise condition rated the sound signals markedly more painful than did subjects in the Mild Noise condition ($p < .001$), indicating that the harm-doing manipulation had been adequate. Next, analysis of variance resulted in no experimental effects on number of sentences written for the partner. Given the wide range of subjects' ages (17 to 65), it seemed possible that age might have influenced responses to the various experimental conditions. Previous research (e.g., Hornstein, 1972; Katz, Cohen, & Glass, 1975) had shown age and altruism to be related—though not in a consistent manner. Hence the sample was split at the median into two age groups: 26 and older, and under 26. The mean age of the older group was 36.9, and of the younger group, 22. A 2 × 2 × 2 (Noise Level × Stigma × Age) analysis of variance was done, with cell Ns ranging from 8 to 14. This revealed a trend toward a three-way interaction effect, $F (1,74) = 3.23$, $p = .07$, suggesting that the two age groups had reacted differently to the Wheelchair and Noise variables.

TABLE 5.3
Mean Number of Sentences Written by Older Subjects
for Disabled and Nondisabled Person
in Noxious and Mild Noise Conditions

	Type of Confederate	
Noise Level	Disabled	Nondisabled
Noxious	38.88 (8)	13.00 (12)
Mild	18.41 (12)	12.30 (9)

Note: Cell *N*s are in parentheses.

To explore the triple interaction, a 2×2 analysis of variance (Stigma $\times$ Noise Level) was done on each age sample. The analysis of younger subjects' helping scores resulted in no effects below the .20 level. But analysis of the older sample's scores showed that significantly more help was given the disabled partner ($M = 28.65$) than the normal one ($M = 12.65$), $F (1,37) = 6.29, p < .02$. Also, there was a tendency for subjects to give more help in the Noxious Noise condition ($M = 25.94$) than in the Mild Noise condition ($M = 15.35$), $F (1,37) = 2.64, p < .11$. Finally, there was a tendency toward a noise by stigma interaction, $F (1,37) = 2.59, p < .12$. The nature of these findings becomes clearer when the cell means (Table 5.3) are inspected. It can be seen that the significant stigma effect was largely confined to the Noxious Noise groups. Comparing these groups, $t (37) = 3.30, p < .01$. In the Mild Noise condition, the difference between the two stigma groups was small, $t (37) = 1.03$. Thus, although the interaction of noise and stigma was not significant, the between-cell comparisons are consistent with the response-amplification prediction.

Other Findings.   Guilt ratings were significantly higher in the Noxious Noise condition than in the Mild Noise condition, $F (1,74) = 7.59, p < .01$. Also, there was a trend toward an interaction of Noise Level and Age on guilt ratings, $F (1,74) = 3.43, p < .07$. Ratings of older women tended to be lower than those of younger women in the Mild Noise condition, and higher in the Noxious Noise condition, suggesting that they were more strongly affected by the noise variable.

Discussion.   The outcome of the experiment was equivocal in that only the behavior of older women was consistent with the response-amplification hypothesis. Possibly, the two age groups had reacted differently to the experience of inflicting loud noise on the partner, with the younger group being less concerned about the partner's discomfort. Or perhaps willingness to help the partner was unduly affected by extraneous factors, such as competing time commitments at the end of the experimental session. Inasmuch as these or other procedural flaws might have been responsible for the ambiguous results, it was decided to do another experiment.

SECOND EXPERIMENT ON HELPING
A HANDICAPPED VICTIM

Subjects were administered a personality test by a graduate research assistant who was either physically disabled or normal. Their responses supposedly were to be used to establish new test norms. Subjects were led to believe either that their test responses had not been candid enough to be usable, thereby creating additional work for the tester, or that their responses had been adequate. Later, all subjects had an opportunity to do a favor for the tester.

Method

The subjects were 57 white nonhandicapped adults, 28 men and 29 women, whose ages ranged from 18 to 68, with a mean of 29. They were recruited through ads in New York City newspapers and paid for participating. Subjects were tested in small groups (usually of four) by a 23-year-old female confederate. Half the time she was seated in a wheelchair, and half the time she appeared nondisabled. She introduced herself as a graduate student who was assisting in the research project, which had as its purpose the development of new norms for a personality test.

Subjects then filled out a 4-item mood scale and an 84-item version of the Bell Adjustment Inventory (a self-description questionnaire). The instructions for the latter stressed the importance of replying honestly. Next, the materials were collected, a 40-item sentence-completion test was distributed, and the tester left the room, ostensibly to do a preliminary scoring of the Bell questionnaires. Returning about 10 minutes later, she announced that one of the subjects had not answered the items on the Adjustment Inventory candidly enough, so the person's questionnaire would have to be discarded and a replacement scheduled.

The confederate explained that the test contained ''lie'' items, dealing with undesirable characteristics that most people have to some extent. If a person consistently denied having these very common negative traits, it was taken as an indication that he or she was not being completely truthful. She concluded ruefully: ''I was hoping this wouldn't happen because I wanted to finish running subjects this week, so that I could get back to my Ph.D. dissertation research.''

The confederate then returned to subjects the copies of the test, mentioning that the project director would collect them later. On the cover of each one, in a box where scores were supposed to be entered, was a handwritten comment. For approximately half the subjects in each group, it read: ''Insufficient self-disclosure. Not usable.'' For the others, the comment was: ''Sufficient self-disclosure. OK.'' Next, subjects filled out a second copy of the mood rating scale, after which the research assistant left the room.

A male faculty member shortly appeared and introduced himself as the project director. He spent a few minutes presenting a fictitious account of the research objectives, collected the test materials, and paid the subjects. As they were getting ready to leave, he mentioned that he would like to make a brief announcement. The Psychology Department, he said, did not have adequate funds to enable graduate students to pay subjects needed for dissertation research. Hence students sometimes asked for permission to recruit volunteers from faculty research projects. Would the subjects mind reading a message by the student who had just tested them? Copies of a printed flier were then distributed. It briefly described a "dissertation research project" on "factors affecting eye–hand coordination" and requested people to indicate whether they would be willing to return to the laboratory at a time convenient for them. If interested, they were to indicate their preference for a ½-hour, 1-hour, 1½-hour, or 2-hour session, and to write their name and telephone number so that they could be called and an appointment arranged. One dollar would be paid for carfare. After allowing enough time for replies, the project director collected the printed forms, debriefed the subjects, and dismissed them.

Results

Helping.   The five possible replies to the appeal for volunteers were scored 0, .5, 1.5, and 2. Experimental effects were assessed by means of a 2 × 2 analysis of variance (Disability × Disclosure). The handicapped tester received significantly larger helping commitments ($M = 1.02$) than the nondisabled one ($M = .68$), $F (1,53) = 4.38$, $p < .05$. Also, there was a nonsignificant tendency for subjects in the Inadequate Self-Disclosure condition to volunteer more help ($M = 1.01$) than did subjects in the Adequate Self-Disclosure condition ($M = .70$), $F (1,53) = 3.24$, $p < .09$. As predicted, there was a significant interaction of Stigma and Harm-doing, $F (1,53) = 4.13$, $p < .05$. The cell means are presented in Table 5.4. In the Inadequate condition, the disabled confederate received more compliance than the normal confederate, $t (53) = 3.82$, $p < .001$, whereas in the Adequate condition, there was no difference in response levels when the confederate was disabled or normal.

Other Findings.   Additional information is provided by the self-ratings of mood. Before and after taking the personality tests and receiving the harm-doing

TABLE 5.4
Mean Compliance Scores in
the Four Stigma/Self-Disclosure Conditions

	Type of Confederate	
Self-Disclosure	Wheelchair	Control
Inadequate	1.36 (14)	.67 (15)
Adequate	.68 (13)	.70 (15)

Note: Cell *N*s are in parentheses.

TABLE 5.5
Cell Means for Changes in Combined Mood Ratings

	Type of Confederate	
Self-Disclosure	Wheelchair	Control
Not adequate	6.75 (12)	1.42 (13)
Adequate	.42 (12)	−1.35 (13)

Note: Cell Ns are in parentheses. The higher the score, the more negative the mood change.

feedback, 50 subjects responded to the following 9-point bipolar scales: relaxed–tense, cheerful–sad, friendly–unfriendly, and confident–lacking in confidence. For each of the scales, prescores in the four experimental conditions were highly similar. The intercorrelations of pre–post change scores on the respective scales within conditions were generally high, two-thirds of them being above .50. Therefore the four scales were combined into a single mood index, and an analysis of variance was done on the composite index change scores. There were two main effects.

For adequacy of self-disclosure, F (1,53) = 16.91, $p < .001$, and for the wheelchair variable, F (1,53) = 5.08, $p < .05$. Although the interaction was not significant—F (1,20) = 2.08, $p < .17$—it can be seen in Table 5.5 that both main effects were due largely to the mood scores of nondisclosers in the Wheelchair group. These subjects showed more negative mood change than did nondisclosers in the Control group, t (20) = 4.93, $p < .001$, whereas the difference between the two stigma groups in the nonharming condition was relatively small and nonsignificant, t (20) = 1.63, $p = .12$.

Correlations were done within conditions between scores on the composite mood index and the helping measure. For Wheelchair/Inadequate, r (10) = .37; for Control/Inadequate, r (11) = .31; $ps > .20$. Correlations were close to zero in the other conditions.

Discussion.   The feedback to subjects about the truthfulness of their self-descriptions on the personality inventory was intended to make them believe that they had or had not done harm to the research assistant by creating additional work for her and thereby disrupting her personal plans. Given the nature of the deception that was used, there appeared to be no feasible way of assessing the adequacy of the harm-doing manipulation or of measuring the amount of guilt experienced by subjects in the two feedback conditions. Hence various alternatives to a guilt interpretation of the mood scores need to be considered. One possibility is that the mood changes reflected anxiety at being told one's test responses were unduly defensive. But it is not apparent why this type of anxiety should have been stronger with a disabled tester than with a normal one (as would have had to be the case if between-treatment differences in mood scores were due to differences in amount of anxiety). Another alternative to a guilt interpretation states that the negative mood changes resulted from subjects' sympathetic iden- tification with the inconvenienced tester. But to account for the pattern of mood scores, this notion would require that people who were told that their test re- sponses were inadequate were more sympathetic than those who were informed that their responses were adequate, even though both groups had the same infor- mation about the tester's plight.

A third possibility is suggested by the general observation that people are unsure of the social norms governing interactions with the disabled, hence tend in mixed encounters to be highly concerned about the appropriateness of their behavior and the kind of impression they are making on others (cf. Davis, 1964; Kleck, 1968). If this is so, subjects may have experienced strong discomfort when given critical feedback by the disabled tester because it meant their be- havior was inappropriate, although not necessarily injurious to the other person. This concept is similar to the guilt notion in its focus on the person's need to avoid negative evaluation. Both ideas provide plausible explanations of the help- ing results: Compliance was highest in the Inadequate Disclosure/Wheelchair condition because of the subject's need to: (1) make restitution for harm-doing as a means of changing *self*-disapproval to approval; or (2) correct a negative self-presentation and thereby change *social* disapproval to approval. We tend to favor the former interpretation, guilt, because it takes account of the fact that subjects were informed explicitly that their action had injured the tester.

GENERAL DISCUSSION

The prediction that unintentional harming would lead to more compensatory helping of stigmatized than of nonstigmatized victims was tested in three experi- ments. In the first study, it was upheld for Black versus White victims. In the second experiment, the response-amplification prediction was upheld for Hand- icapped versus Control victims only among older subjects, following the post- hoc introduction of an Age variable. There appears to be no satisfactory explana- tion of this Age effect, although an additional finding that the Noise variable had somewhat more impact on the older group's reported feelings is perhaps a clue. The data from the third experiment are consistent with the helping prediction as applied to handicapped victims, but the manipulation of harm-doing was perhaps not as clean as in the first two investigations.

Taken in conjunction with the findings presented in Chapter 4, these results support the notion that people's behavior toward those whom they have uninten- tionally injured is likely to be more extreme when the victims are black or disabled than when they are members of the majority group. Only fragmentary support was found for the assumption that response amplification is mediated by guilt arousal. In the first study, subjects reported feeling more guilt over hurting the black partner than the white one, and in the third study, there was more negative change in mood ratings after subjects presumably had harmed a disabled as compared with a control confederate. In none of the experiments did correlational analyses provide clear evidence of affective mediation. However, as mentioned earlier, the guilt state seems to be extremely difficult to measure (cf. Freedman, 1970). Not the least important reason is that people may deny guilt as a means of coping with it. Moreover, in Experiments 1 and 2, guilt ratings were obtained after subjects had the opportunity to reduce their guilt by behaving altruistically.

6 A Reverse Tokenism Effect

According to the ambivalence-amplification model, doing a favor for a member of a stigmatized group may arouse psychic tension in the actor because the friendly action contradicts the hostile, disvaluing component of his ambivalent attitude toward people like the recipient. He may feel that he has displayed excessive sympathy for an unworthy object or that he has put himself out for the other person for irrelevant reasons. These cognitions may pose a threat to the actor's self-image as a judicious and fair-minded person. The ensuing attempt to reduce inner conflict may take the form of extreme behavior toward the other person, either positive or negative depending on the circumstances. In this chapter, I am concerned with the positive side of this hypothesis. Studies are presented that test the prediction that doing a favor for a stigmatized stranger will have a more favorable effect on subsequent behavior toward him than will doing a favor for a nonstigmatized person.

Of some relevance is the "foot-in-the-door" phenomenon, first demonstrated by Freedman and Fraser (1966), in which meeting a small request increases the likelihood that one will later meet a larger request. Freedman and Fraser showed, for example, that people who promised to display a small sign reading "Keep California Beautiful" in a window of their home were at another time more willing than a one-contact control group to have a large, unsightly sign bearing the same or a different public interest message put up on their front lawn. The effect occurred even when the second request was made by a different person. This finding has since been replicated by several investigators, including Pliner, Hart, Kohl, and Saari (1974), Snyder and Cunningham (1975), and Seligman, Bush, and Kirsch (1976).

However, the foot-in-the-door research has been limited in two ways. First, except in a study by Uranowitz (1975), the kind of help requested has always been quite impersonal, having to do more with support for charitable and public interest enterprises than with gratification of the needs of the help-seeker. It is entirely possible that doing a *personal* favor for someone about whom one has neither positive nor negative feelings will tend to reduce one's willingness to do him another favor, because of psychological reactance (Brehm, 1966). Another limitation of this research is that investigators have not considered how characteristics of the help-seeker may act to strengthen or dampen the foot-in-the-door effect.

Other considerations suggest that helping may lead to greater liking of the recipient. According to Bem's (1967) self-perception theory, a person who observes himself voluntarily benefiting another may infer that he likes the other. Dissonance theory leads to the same conclusion, especially for situations where the beneficiary is initially disliked. Common sense, of course, would say that as attraction to a person increases, so also does one's willingness to aid him. As yet, little research has been done on the nature of the relationship between helping and liking. There is slight support for: (1) the notion that helping enhances liking for the recipient, from studies by Jecker and Landy (1969), and Schopler and Compere (1971); and (2) the notion that helping is facilitated by liking, from a study by Gross, Wallston, and Piliavin (1975).

To find out whether stigma can enhance the effect of an altruistic action on future responses to the benefited person, two studies were carried out. In both, the stigma variation consisted of having a help-seeker who was either physically disabled or normal. The first study was done by this author and Timothy Emswiller and has not been reported elsewhere.

FIRST EXPERIMENT ON EFFECT OF HELPING A DISABLED PERSON

Method

Fifty-one nonhandicapped adults, 19 men and 32 women aged 21 to 60, were recruited through an ad in a New York City newspaper and paid for attending a single session. They were tested in groups of two or three by a young male adult who for half of the sessions was seated in a wheelchair and for half was physically normal. The tester introduced himself as a graduate research assistant and explained to subjects that they would be working on verbal tasks that were being developed for use in future research. Each person was given a booklet containing three moderately interesting, affectively neutral tasks with self-administering instructions, and sent to separate testing rooms where they worked alone for 25 minutes. Then the tester went to each room to present the next task, the instructions for which constituted the manipulation of the second independent variable.

Half of the subjects were in an Induced Helping condition. They were told that a second booklet had not been delivered as promised by the duplicating shop. Hence, no further testing could be done—the person was free to leave and would be paid for a full session. But inasmuch as the subject had expected to remain an hour, the tester wished to ask a personal favor: Would the participant be willing to help him on his Ph.D. dissertation research by working at a simple paper-and-pencil task for about 10 minutes? The research ostensibly dealt with the effect of response repetition on motor coordination. All subjects in the Induced Helping condition complied with the request and were given a booklet that contained several blank pages and instructions to write a brief specimen sentence repeatedly until told to stop. Half of the subjects were in a No Induced Helping condition. Instead of being told that the second test booklet had not arrived, and asked to do the handwriting task as a favor to the confederate, they were given the task as though it was part of the work for which they were being paid.

Ten minutes later, in both conditions, the confederate returned to the individual testing rooms, collected the materials, and sent the subjects back to the main laboratory, where a male faculty member introduced himself as the project director and directed subjects to chairs spaced several feet apart from one another. He gave a brief fictitious account of the research objectives and then paid them. From this point on, the procedure was the same as the one used to measure willingness to help the confederate in the third experiment presented in Chapter 5 (the inadequate self-disclosure experiment). That is, the "project director" distributed a printed announcement supposedly prepared by the confederate to enlist volunteers for his dissertation research. Those who were interested were to check their preference for a ½-hour, 1-hour, 1½-hour, or 2-hour session, and to write in their names and telephone numbers so that they could be called and an appointment arranged; one dollar would be paid for carfare. After the experimenter had collected the completed forms, he debriefed the subjects and dismissed them.

Results and Discussion

The number of times subjects wrote the eight-word specimen sentence provides a check on the constancy of performance at the handwriting task across the four Disability $\times$ Induced Helping conditions. The various cell means were all very similar (combined mean of 45.5), indicating that the confederate's initial request for help elicited the same amount of effort in both the Wheelchair and Control conditions as did the tester's instructions to perform the task as part of the paid work.

The dependent variable was the amount of time subjects said they would be willing to devote to the tester's research, scored from 0 to 2. A 2×2 analysis of

TABLE 6.1
Mean Time Commitments in the Four Stigma/Prior-Help
Conditions of the First Experiment

| Condition | Type of Confederate | |
	Wheelchair	Control
Prior Helping	1.29 (12)	.50 (13)
No Prior Helping	.73 (13)	.92 (13)

Note: Cell Ns are in parentheses.

variance resulted in a significant interaction, F (1,47) = 5.48, p = .02, as depicted in Table 6.1. When a prior helping request had not been made, subjects made slightly larger time commitments in the Control than in the Wheelchair condition, t (47) < 1.0. But after the initial compliance experience, responsiveness to the later request was significantly higher in the Wheelchair than in the Control condition, t (47) = 2.68, p < .02. The somewhat negative effect of prior helping in the Control condition perhaps reflects psychological reactance (Brehm, 1966). Thus the results—a kind of amplified foot-in-the-door effect when the help-seeker was handicapped—were generally supportive of the prediction from the ambivalence model. It seemed desirable to do a conceptual replication, using better safeguards against possible subject contamination and experimenter bias effects. The new experiment, which has not been reported elsewhere, was carried out by this author and Saul Podhorzer.

SECOND EXPERIMENT ON EFFECT OF
HELPING A DISABLED PERSON

Method

The subjects were 36 students from a college in New York City, 20 men and 16 women, who were recruited through an ad in the campus newspaper and paid for attending one session. The procedure used in the first part of the session was similar to that of the prior experiment. That is, a young male adult who either was or was not confined to a wheelchair presented the "test development" cover story to groups of four or five subjects and then administered a series of verbal tasks. However, there were a few procedural differences: (1) a different person played the role of test administrator; (2) subjects remained in the same room while working at the tasks, visually separated by wooden partitions, instead of being sent to separate rooms; and (3) they sat facing the tester, who timed each task with a stopwatch, announcing when to start and stop.

This phase took about 35 minutes. When the tasks had been completed, the tester collected the test booklets and left the room. Shortly thereafter the experimenter entered, introduced himself as the project director, and gave the same fictitious debriefing that had been used in the prior study. At this point, the second independent variable was introduced. Groups in the Prior Helping condition were told that the graduate student who had tested them was being considered for a regular appointment as a research assistant. The experimenter explained that the most important qualification for the job was the ability to put subjects at ease, to establish rapport, so they would perform at their highest level; therefore it was very useful to get evaluative input from subjects before making the permanent job assignment. The confidentiality of replies was emphasized. Then an evaluation form was distributed. In the Prior Helping condition, it stated in part: "If you wish to recommend this person for a position as a Research Assistant, please write in the space below why you think he or she would be a good test administrator. For example, you might want to state whether the person . . . gave clear instructions, was efficient, has a warm and friendly manner . . . "

In the No Prior Helping condition, the evaluation form requested the subject to state any reasons why the confederate should not be given the assistantship. "For example, you might feel that he or she was careless and inefficient . . . not sincerely interested in the project, not able to give clear instructions . . . . " (The reason for providing an ostensible opportunity for negative evaluation was to hold constant across both conditions the information that subjects received about the job status of the confederate. It was expected that no comments, negative or otherwise, would be written by subjects in the No Prior Helping condition.)

In both conditions, subjects returned the forms in sealed envelopes addressed to the project director. Next, the dependent variable was introduced, following the method of the earlier study: After subjects had been paid, they were given a printed announcement, supposedly prepared by the confederate, asking them to return to the laboratory at a future time to participate in his dissertation research without pay; the amount of time they promised to give him (no time, ½ hour, 1 hour, 1½ hours, 2 hours) was the measure of helping commitment. Following this, subjects filled out a postexperimental questionnaire and were fully debriefed.

Results

As a check on the adequacy of the prior-helping manipulation, subjects were given a two-item questionnaire at the end of the experimental session asking whether they believed their recommendations would: (1) influence the hiring decision; and (2) help the confederate to get the job. Replies were made on 4-point scales ranging from "definitely would . . . " to "definitely would not . . . . " On both items, the scores of the Prior Helping groups were more affirmative than those of the No Prior Helping groups. Analysis of variance showed that only the prior helping main effects were significant ($ps < .01$). As a further check, subjects' written comments on the evaluation forms were examined. In the Prior Helping/Wheelchair and Prior Helping/Control conditions,

TABLE 6.2
Mean Time Commitments in the Four Stigma/Prior-Help
Conditions of the Second Experiment

	Type of Confederate	
Condition	Wheelchair	Control
Prior Helping	1.38	.33
No Prior Helping	.33	.77

Note: N = 9 in all cells.

every subject wrote at least two lines of comments (all favorable); the means were 5.4 and 4.7, respectively. In the two No Prior Helping conditions, the corresponding means were 0 and .17. Here, too, there were no negative comments. Thus the manipulation apparently was adequate in that Prior Helping subjects all wrote favorable evaluations that they reported believing would help the confederate, whereas No Prior Helping subjects wrote virtually no comments and seemed not to feel that their returned evaluation forms would help the confederate.

Turning to the main finding, analysis of variance of the commitment scores resulted in one effect, a highly significant interaction of the disability and prior helping variables, $F = 14.70$, $p < .001$; cell means are presented in Table 6.2. When there was no prior experience of aiding the confederate, subjects in the Control condition made slightly larger time commitments than did subjects in the Wheelchair condition, t (32) < 1.0. But subjects who had an initial experience of aiding the disabled tester made significantly larger commitments to participate in his research than did those in either the No Prior Helping/Wheelchair or the Prior Helping/Normal conditions; for both comparisons, t (32) $= 3.68$, $p < .001$.

GENERAL DISCUSSION

The results of the second study show even more strongly than those of the first that doing a favor for a handicapped person as compared with doing one for a normal counterpart may have a more favorable effect on subsequent responsiveness to the help-seeker's needs. In fact, when the help-seeker was normal, the first benevolent action did not in any way enhance willingness to meet a later request. There was even the suggestion of a small negative effect. The findings run counter to the tokenism phenomenon, which Dutton and Lennox (1974) define as the tendency of the majority to make small concessions to members of stigmatized groups in order to avoid having to make larger, more costly ones.

However, the present findings must be viewed with caution, and alternatives to an altruistic interpretation considered. For instance, in the second experiment, subjects who had written favorable evaluations may have volunteered to return so that they could inform the confederate that they had supported his job application, hoping thereby to elicit an expression of gratitude, which perhaps would be seen as especially flattering when it came from a member of a rejected group. This "seeking-of-praise" interpretation is not compelling, yet it cannot be ruled out on the basis of the available evidence. The role of ambivalence as a mediator of the enhanced helping effect is also unclear, since attitude toward the disabled was not measured. Perhaps sympathy alone rather than ambivalence underlay the observed behavior toward the disabled stimulus person. But a sympathy assumption sould seem to imply a main effect of disability, not the disability by prior helping interaction that actually occurred.

7 Some Stimulus Factors in Cross-Racial Helping

This chapter deals with some factors other than white people's prior behavior toward a black help-seeker that determine their willingness to befriend him. Three field studies by Katz, Cohen, and Glass (1975) are presented, and the results are discussed in relation to some other recent investigations of cross-racial altruism.

In a number of earlier studies done in the United States, white subjects tended to reject blacks' request for aid (e.g., Bryan & Test, 1967; Gaertner, 1973; Gaertner & Bickman, 1971; Graf & Ridell, 1972; West, Whitney, & Schnedler, 1975); whereas in other studies, there were no reliable differences in the racial targeting of assistance (Hornstein, 1972; Lerner, Solomon, & Brody, 1971; Piliavin, Rodin, & Piliavin, 1969; Wispé & Freshley, 1971). In contrast to these findings, Dutton (1973) reported that Canadian whites gave more frequent and generally larger donations to black and Indian solicitors for a nonethnic charity than they gave to white solicitors. Interestingly, Dutton's was the only experiment in which confederates actively sought aid in pursuit of a socially valued goal. (One American study, Bryan and Test's, used a charity appeal, but this investigation was not comparable to Dutton's because the confederates, who posed as attendants of Salvation Army kettles, were not allowed to speak to potential donors or to make eye contact with them.)

Seeking contributions for a worthy nonethnic philanthropy is generally regarded as an activity that benefits society as a whole and therefore deserves to be encouraged and supported. Giving money could have the meaning for the donor not only of aiding a particular charity but also of expressing approval of the solicitor. The ambivalence-amplification interpretation of Dutton's results would be that when nonwhites were seen to be engaged in a socially valued humanitarian effort, white observers had a need to show their lack of bigotry, which they did by means of an amplified compliance response. (In the theoretical model presented in Chapter 3, this would be the situation of positive initial input by a stigmatized other.) If this view is correct, it should operate not only when the confederate's goal is humanitarian but also when aid is sought in support of more personal goals that are strongly approved in white society—for example, the achievement goals embodied in the Protestant work ethic. In the first field study done by Katz, Cohen, and Glass, black and white confederates, who presented themselves as college students who were working their way through college, requested white subjects to take part in a brief consumer-survey interview. The prediction was that black canvassers would receive more compliance than white canvassers.

It was also anticipated that compliance rates might be affected by the manner in which aid was solicited. Favoring of black help-seekers should be more likely to occur when the solicitor adheres to conventional norms of courtesy (positive self-presentation), whereas the opposite outcome—i.e., relative rejection of blacks—should be more likely when the solicitor seems to violate these norms by being unduly assertive or by seeming to take for granted the other's cooperation (negative self-presentation).

Further, the minority person's mode of self-reference might influence the white subject's responsiveness. In 1973, when the studies were done, the term *black*, as compared with *Negro*, probably suggested to many whites a more critical and less conforming attitude toward the main society because of its association with minority protest. Therefore the person who identified himself as *black* might elicit less assistance than one who used the word *Negro*. This seemed a plausible prediction, since most subjects were from a white population known to have relatively conventional racial views—middle and lower-middle-income males past age 30 (cf. Campbell, 1971). Finally, the research included a measure of racial attitude that it was hoped would be useful in evaluating motives for cross-racial helping.

THE TELEPHONE EXPERIMENT

Method

The subjects were 2340 male adults living in middle- and lower-middle-income, virtually 100% white, residential blocks in New York City. Names from voter registration lists were randomly assigned to 18 treatments, representing all combinations of the following conditions: three levels of help-seeker's assertiveness, three types of help-seeker's racial identification, and two confederates acting as help-seekers. Two male college students, one black and the other white, contacted subjects by telephone on weekday evenings, using every combination of experimental conditions an equal number of times. When subjects in the Low Assertiveness condition answered the telephone, the caller said:

> Hello Mr.--------. My name is David Clark. I am in the [racial identification] Students' Self-Help Program at the City College of New York, and I have a part-time job doing consumer attitude surveys. Would you mind answering a few questions about men's shoes? It will take about five minutes of your time.

The Medium Assertiveness script was the same, except that instead of the words "Would you mind . . . " the phrase "I'm sure you won't mind . . . " was used. High Assertiveness was the same as Low Assertiveness, except that in place of the last two sentences, the following was substituted: "I'm sure you can give me five minutes of your time. I want you to answer some questions about men's shoes." Racial identification was manipulated independently of assertiveness by inserting either *Negro, black,* or no label in the script, where indicated above. It was assumed that when no label was used, the caller would be perceived as white.[1]

The dependent variable was the subject's stated willingness or refusal to be interviewed. If he assented, the confederate terminated the call by asking a "filter" question that "disqualified" him as a respondent, thanked him, and hung up.

The attitudinal phase of the research began 1 month later. Samples of compliers and noncompliers were randomly selected from each of the following treatments: Black/High Assertion, Negro/High Assertion, Negro/Low Assertion, and White/Low Assertion.[2] Under the guise of conducting an opinion poll, two new male confederates, both white, called these subjects and requested that they answer some questions about a variety of local political issues connected with an impending mayoralty election. Embedded in the interview were six items about the causes of minority people's job, educational, and housing problems, which pitted situational (discrimination, lack of opportunity) against dispositional (personal inadequacy) explanations.[3] Over 70% of the helpers and a similar percentage of the nonhelpers who were called back for the attitude interview were successfully interviewed.

---

[1] As a check on this assumption, a tape recording of the black confederate reading the No Label/Low Assertiveness script was played to 20 white males who were unacquainted with the research. They then filled out a "voice impression" questionnaire in which an ethnic identity item was embedded. All 20 subjects falsely identified the speaker as white.

[2] Because of the time lapse between the two calls, it was assumed that subjects' responses to the first call would not influence their attitudinal replies. Inasmuch as the attitude data were supposed to shed light on the motivation for favoring minority help-seekers, the Negro condition—where such favoring occurred—was sampled extensively. Attitude-helping relationships were not anticipated in the Black and No Label conditions.

[3] The internal consistency of the six items, as estimated by Cronbach's Coefficient Alpha, was .49 ($N = 160$).

Results

The helping scores (i.e., compliance or noncompliance) were analyzed by means of a 3 × 3 × 2 (Level of Assertiveness × Racial Identification × Confederates) analysis of variance, with 130 subjects per cell. Helping rates for the various conditions are expressed here as percentages rather than as means. All three main effects, but none of the interactions, were significant.

For the two confederates, the respective levels of helping were 55.1% and 65.5%, F (1,2322) = 18.65, $p <$ .001. The higher rate of helping was obtained by the black caller. Because there was no statistical interaction of confederates with racial identification or assertiveness, and because (as already mentioned) an independent check had shown that in the No Label condition the black confederate's voice was perceived as that of a white person, it seems justifiable to regard the differential effectiveness of the two confederates as a personality phenomenon unrelated to the hypotheses of the experiment. Figure 7.1 summarizes the results for the other variables.

Helping scores in the three racial identification conditions were as follows: Negro, 65.0%; White (i.e., No Label) 58.8%; and Black, 57.1%, F (1,2322) = 5.90, $p <$ .01. Between-levels comparisons revealed, as predicted, that the Negro compliance rate was significantly higher than that for White (t = 2.55, $p <$ .02) and Black (t = 3.24, $p <$ .002).

The assertion variable had a fairly linear effect on helping: Low Assertiveness, 68.9%; Medium Assertiveness, 62.3%; and High Assertiveness, 54.5%; F (2,2322) = 27.40, $p <$ .001). The predicted interaction of racial identification and assertiveness was not significant; however, there appeared to be some tendency toward a convergence of Negro and White helping scores as assertiveness increased. In the Low Assertion condition, compliance scores for the Negro and white help seekers were 74.6% and 63.1%, respectively (t = 2.85, $p <$ .01), whereas for Medium and High Assertion, the differences were progressively smaller and nonsignificant (65.1% versus 59.6%, and 55.4% versus 53.5%, respectively). These comparisons provide some support for the prediction that relatively high assertiveness would be more detrimental to the minority help-seeker than to the white help-seeker.

Turning to the relation between racial attitude and helping, point biserial correlations were computed between attitude favorability scores and compliance in the Negro/Low Assertion (N = 78) and Negro/High Assertion (N = 82) conditions. The correlations were − .32 ($p <$ .01) and − .20 ($p <$ .10). That is, the more favorable the attitude, the less likelihood there was of compliance. Attitude and helping were not related to one another in two other conditions where attitude scores were obtained, White/Low Assertion (N = 40) and Black/High Assertion (N = 70). Thus a significant association between attitude and helping was found only in the condition where the self-presentation of the minority help-seeker was most favorable—i.e., where a pro-minority bias in compliance had been theoretically expected and had been obtained.

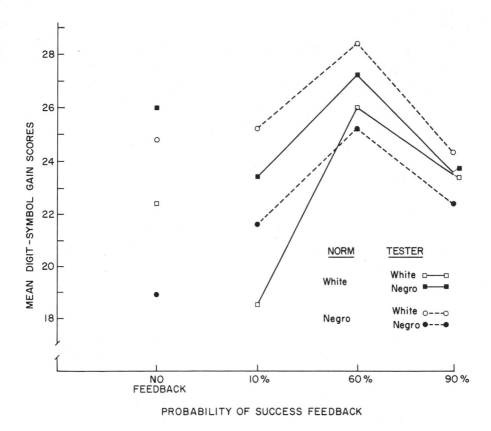

FIG. 7.1. Percent compliance for both confederates combined in the various assertiveness × racial identification treatments. ($N = 260$ for every treatment.)

THE SUBWAY INTERVIEW EXPERIMENT

The previous experiment showed that the manipulation of racial cues by means of verbal labels had certain predicted effects on helpfulness in a telephone situation. A question arises as to whether a minority person would receive favored treatment in a face-to-face situation where the racial cues were the physical characteristics of the help-seeker, and where compliance entailed direct social contact. Accordingly, a new experiment was done in subway stations. Given the racially mixed population of the stations, it seemed appropriate to use both black and white subjects. Also, to further explore the social desirability notion, a status-of-confederate variable was substituted for the verbal–label and assertiveness variables of the first experiment.

Method

Subjects were 960 male adults who were waiting for trains on subway station platforms. They were approached by confederates posing as hired interviewers and asked to answer some questions about a consumer product. Six new confederates were used, three black and three white, all between the ages of 22 and 27. They were dressed neatly and carried a clipboard and pencil. The independent variables were as follows: Race of Subjects, Race of Confederates, Age of Subjects, and ostensible educational Status of Confederates. The same number of subjects were used in every combination of conditions.

The experiment was run during weekday off-rush hours in two large subway stations in mid-Manhattan. Only one confederate worked a station at a given time. Starting at one end of a two-track platform, he approached Black and Caucasian men who appeared to be at least 18 years of age and were standing alone. The confederate made an estimate of each subject's age as being under 30 or 30 or older. Confederates' estimates showed agreement of 90% or higher with estimates made by one of the investigators.

A systematic sampling procedure was followed whereby the man standing closest to every second pillar on alternate sides of the platform was contacted, provided a train was not standing or approaching on either side. In the High Status condition, the confederate identified himself as a college student working for a marketing research company in his spare time. Would the subject be willing to spend a few minutes answering some questions about cleaning fluid? In the Low Status condition, the reference to being a student was omitted. If the subject replied that he was afraid he might miss his train, the confederate assured him that the interview would be broken off if necessary. Subjects who complied were then asked a "filter" question that "disqualified" them as respondents, and the contact was terminated.

Results

Data of the three black confederates and of the three white confederates, respectively, were pooled. Then a $2 \times 2 \times 2 \times 2$ analysis of variance was done on the helping scores (Race of Subject $\times$ Age of Subject $\times$ Race of Confederate $\times$ Status of Confederate). There were 60 subjects in every cell, and for all effects to be reported $df = 1$ and 944.

The most important finding was a main effect of Race of Confederate: 84.6% of subjects helped black confederates, and 68.5% helped white confederates ($F = 37.24$, $p < .001$). Next, High Status confederates elicited more compliance (79.6%) than Low Status confederates (73.3%). For the difference $F = 5.80$, $p < .025$. There was also a main effect of Age ($F = 64.48$, $p < .001$), with young subjects complying more (86.8%) than old subjects (66.4%).

In addition, there were two interaction effects involving confederates, for which the helping scores are shown in Table 7.1. Age of Subjects interacted with

TABLE 7.1
Compliance Percentages in Subway Interview
Experiment for Two Interaction Effects

Age of Subject × *Race of Confederate*		
	Young Subjects	*Old Subjects*
White confederate	81.7	55.4
Black confederate	92.1	76.7

Status of Confederate × *Race of Confederate*		
	High Status	*Low Status*
White confederate	69.2	67.9
Black confederate	90.0	78.7

Note: $N = 240$ in all cells.

Race of Confederates ($F = 4.36$, $p < .05$): The effect of age was stronger for white confederates than for black confederates. Also, there was a nearly significant interaction of confederates' status and confederates' race ($F = 3.71$, $p < .06$), indicating that the black confederates produced almost the entire main effect for status.

Given the high incidence of violent crime in the subways, and the belief of many people that most of the crimes are perpetrated by minority youths, it is conceivable that subjects complied with the black confederates' request as much out of fear as for more positive reasons. This possibility might be seen as damaging to an interpretation of the results in terms of the perceived social desirability of the help-seeker's behavior. Therefore, another experiment was carried out, in which the fear potential was at least as strong as in this study, but the nature of the confederates' request did not suggest that favoring of blacks should occur.

THE CHANGE-FOR-A-QUARTER EXPERIMENT

Method

This study was done in the same subway stations as the previous study; it had 800 subjects, equally divided into age and racial groups. Three black and three white confederates were used, of whom five had been used in the prior study. The sampling procedure was the same as in the prior study. Also, as in the prior study, they were attired in a neat, middle-class manner. The confederate approached each subject by saying: "Excuse me, do you have change for a quarter?" As he said this, he held out his hand with a quarter in the upturned palm.

The subject was judged to have complied with the request if he reached into his pocket and brought out coins for inspection. It was assumed that most subjects would not know exactly how much change they had with them, so that a negative reply without searching would be tantamount to a rejection. If the subject offered change for the quarter, the confederate completed the exchange, thanked him, and moved on. If not, he was also thanked, and the confederate moved on.

Results

The helping scores were evaluated by means of a $2 \times 2 \times 2$ analysis of variance (Race of Subject $\times$ Age of Subject $\times$ Race of Confederate), with 100 subjects per cell. There was one strong effect: White confederates received more help (54.5%) than black confederates (38.3%), with $F (1,792) = 20.48$, $p < .001$. Also, there was a weak tendency for whites to comply more than blacks. The respective rates were 49.0% and 43.8%, $F (1,792) = 2.73$, $p < .10$.

GENERAL DISCUSSION

The results show that minority help-seekers were favored over whites when both displayed the same socially desirable characteristics, and that pro-minority bias tended to diminish as the self-presentations of both black and white help-seekers became less positive. Thus, as confederates in the telephone experiment became increasingly assertive, there was less tendency to favor the Negro caller over the white caller. The fact that assertiveness adversely affected compliance rates across all three types of racial identification underscores the reasonableness of the interpretation that a norm of courtesy was being violated. Another variation in the telephone study that can be linked to social desirability was black versus Negro self-identification. The label *black* did not elicit the same favored treatment as the term *Negro*. This was predicted on the assumption that for many subjects *black,* as compared with *Negro*, would imply a more critical and less conforming orientation toward white norms and values.[4]

Social desirability seems also to account for the interaction effect of interviewer's race and educational status on compliance in the subway interview experiment. Favoring of the black confederate was twice as great in the College Student condition as in the Nonstudent condition. Working one's way through college is a time-honored cliché of the Protestant ethic, American style, which apparently still evokes an image of commendable achievement striving.

Finally, in the one situation where white help-seekers were significantly more successful than blacks—asking for change for a quarter—the confederate exhib-

---

[4]A survey of black Americans' attitudes by Schuman and Hatchett (1974) indicates that this was an accurate perception at the time.

ited no strongly positive characteristics and was not visibly engaged in a socially valued activity. However, given the concern about subway crime in New York, subjects may have been fearful of being bilked, robbed, or aggressively panhandled when asked by a stranger to display money. But despite this element of ambiguity in the last experiment, the overall pattern of results in all three studies supports the social-desirability interpretation.

There seems to be a number of plausible reasons why social desirability led to the favoring of black solicitors in the first two experiments. First, favorable perceptions of their behavior may have aroused latent sympathy for the minority-group underdog, which was then expressed altruistically. Another possibility arises from the fact that many white people perceive segments of the black population as being alienated from, and even hostile to, white values and norms (cf. Campbell, 1971) and thereby potentially threatening to the security and well-being of the majority group. Hence, self-interest alone may have disposed the white person to reinforce black behavior that showed support for his values (cf. Hornstein's, 1972, notion of promotive tension).

More complex than either of the foregoing one-factor suggestions is the idea that the racial attitudes of white subjects tended to be ambivalent, so that when confronted with minority behavior that challenged their negative beliefs about the group, many of them experienced a need to defend their self-image as unprejudiced individuals. Thus, in Dutton's (1973) experiment, where nonwhites were seen to be engaged in socially valued humanitarian activity, the ambivalent subject was presumably vulnerable to self-accusations of bigotry, and the threat was resolved through suppression of antagonistic feelings and enhancement of friendly, sympathetic feelings. The result was an amplified helping response.

The three suggested motives for favoring black help-seekers—to reinforce conformity behavior, to express sympathy per se, and to defend self-esteem against ambivalence-induced threat—are all intuitively plausible. However, the notion of an unambivalent sympathy motive is discredited by the evidence from the attitude scores, which shows that subjects who complied with the Negro caller's request were more inclined than noncompliers to attribute the special problems of blacks to their personal inadequacies rather than to objective barriers to achievement.[5] But this tendency of compliers to criticize the black group is consistent with the idea of a motive to reinforce socially desirable behavior in members of a group perceived as alienated from white norms and values. It is also compatible with the ambivalence assumption. An ambivalence interpretation of the results of the first experiment would state that the criticism of blacks in general and the favorable response to the help-seeker who used the label *Negro*

---

[5]Interestingly, the mean racial attitude score for all subjects tested was on the negative side of the scale. Answers to all items revealed a generally conservative outlook. For example, on a question about how to deal with the problem of street crime, a large majority—67%—advocated a "get-tough" policy of more arrests and stiffer jail sentences, whereas only 33% felt that it was at least equally important to provide better job and educational opportunities for the poor.

were convenient, low-cost modes of resolving attitudinal conflict in different settings. The "political poll" provided an opportunity to justify one's dislike of blacks in general without completely ruling out the possibility of sympathy, whereas granting the small request of an individual black with positive traits was an easy way to express sympathy and prove one's fair-mindedness without having to disavow critical beliefs about the group as a whole.

To test the ambivalence interpretation further, a new study was done by Irwin Katz, David Glass, & David Lucido in which white adults filled out a racial attitude questionnaire based on Kaplan's (1972) technique for measuring ambivalence and later were requested to sign a pro-minority petition.

THE PETITION STUDY

Method

The subjects were 109 white men and women, ranging in age from 17 to 65, who responded to an ad in a New York City newspaper offering $5 for filling out a set of psychological questionnaires. The battery of tests included personality questionnaires and a modified version of Kaplan's unipolar evaluative scales for the concepts *black people* and *white people*. The Kaplan instrument consisted of 16 unipolar 6-point (0–5) evaluative scales, of which 8 had positive trait labels and 8 had polar opposite labels. Ambivalence was defined as total affect minus unambivalent affect, where total affect was the sum of the positive scale ratings plus the sum of the negative scale ratings, and unambivalent affect was the difference between the sums of the positive and negative ratings, disregarding sign.[6]

A few months after the questionnaires had been administered, each subject received a mail solicitation, ostensibly from an organization of "Negro college students," urging him or her to sign and mail back a petition. The petition was directed to the mayor and urged him to continue a city-sponsored program that was threatened with termination. The program provided emergency aid to slum tenants who could not get their landlords to make essential repairs in their apartments.

Results

Copies of the letter to the mayor were signed and returned by 43.6% of the men ($N = 58$) and 42.6% of the women ($N = 51$). There were no age or educational differences between compliers and noncompliers. With respect to the racial attitude measures, the product moment correlation between the positive and

---

[6]It was decided to use the Kaplan scales rather than the racial prejudice and sympathy scales that had been used in our earlier study of harm-doing and denigration (Chapter 4) because the latter measures seemed to have become somewhat outdated.

negative scale ratings for the concept *black people* was a low .13, indicating that evaluations of favorable and unfavorable characteristics were largely independent of one another. To see whether ambivalence about blacks was related to compliance behavior, the point biserial correlation between these measures was computed, resulting in a value of .40 ($p < .001$). Thus the theoretical prediction was supported. Also, as expected, the point biserial correlation between ambivalence about white people and helping was close to zero.

For the ratings of black people, the product moment correlation between ambivalence and scores on the positive scales was .69, and between ambivalence and scores on the negative scales it was .68 ($ps < .001$), indicating that both the positive and negative ratings contributed substantially to the composite ambivalence score. Next, the relationship between each of these component attitudes and helping behavior was assessed, resulting in a point biserial correlation of .26 ($p < .01$) for helping and positive scale scores (the higher the positive score, the more helping), and a correlation of .18 ($p < .10$) for helping and negative scale scores (the higher the negative score, the more helping).

Of the various personality measures included in the test battery—Mehrabian's (1972) Measure of Empathic Tendency, Crowne and Marlowe's (1964) Social Desirability, and Taylor's (1953) Manifest Anxiety Scale—none was related to helping behavior or to any of the racial attitude indices.

Overall, empirical support for the ambivalence hypothesis must be regarded as somewhat equivocal. Our index of ambivalence—the sum of the positive and negative trait ratings minus the difference between them—correlated substantially with the respective positive and negative scale scores. Furthermore, the positive scale scores alone were significantly related to helping behavior. Therefore the possibility exists that the relationship between the ambivalence index and helping was to some extent a scoring artifact.

RELATED RESEARCH

Status Effects

It would seem that the white majority may be willing to encourage the achievement efforts of blacks, when these efforts are in conformity with the dominant norms. However, a study by Benson, Karabenick, and Lerner (1976) suggests that many whites react unfavorably when members of the minority group pursue prestigious educational and vocational goals that have traditionally been exclusively white. White adult callers in public telephone booths found a completed application form for admission to a graduate psychology program at a major northern university. Included with the application was a photograph that established the candidate's racial identity, and an addressed, stamped envelope. People were more likely to mail the application of a white than of a black candidate. The difference in the proportion of helpers was not large (45% vs.

37%), but it was statistically significant. Thus there was a bias against helping blacks, in contrast to the pro-black tendency shown by subjects in the consumer-survey experiments described earlier.

◦ The inconsistency may merely reflect a difference in the procedures employed. Inasmuch as people in the lost application study did not interact with the person in need of help, fear of censure was not a factor that could influence their behavior. But although social interaction was present in both of the consumer-survey experiments, it probably was not a critical determinant of compliance in the first experiment, where communication was by telephone. Another difference between the lost application and consumer-survey studies was that in the former, the person in need of assistance was pursuing a higher achievement goal—i.e., an advanced degree in psychology as compared with graduation from college or holding a job as a market-survey interviewer. It may be that many whites perceive blacks as qualified to attend college or hold ordinary white collar jobs but as lacking the academic competence for high-level professional training at predominantly white institutions.

An experiment by Dovidio and Gaertner (1977) deals directly with the status factor in cross-racial helping. In this study, white subjects had an opportunity to do a favor for a black confederate whose role status in the situation was either higher or lower than their own. Male college students were assigned to work on group tasks, supposedly requiring abstract intelligence, with a black or white confederate posing as a fellow subject. One person was designated to be the "supervisor" and the other the "worker." Before the men began working on the first task, the partner "accidentally" knocked over a container filled with pencils, scattering them on the floor. Overall, subjects were more likely to help the black partner pick up the pencils than they were to help the white partner. However, this effect was qualified by a Race × Role interaction effect: When the confederate had the subordinate role, the black partner was helped twice as often as the white one (83% vs. 42%), but when the confederate was the supervisor, the pro-black bias of subjects virtually disappeared (58% vs. 54%).

The studies I have reviewed in this chapter indicate that status factors may have an important influence on the dominant group's reactions to minority members. The pro-black discrimination that was observed by Katz et al. (1975) appears to be a phenomenon most likely to occur when the status and power goals perceived to be pursued or already occupied by black help-seekers: (1) accord with the white observer's view of their competence; and (2) do not threaten his own status and power needs.

Diffusion of Responsibility

That diffusion of responsibility is a factor that can influence white people's responsiveness to the plight of minority individuals has been shown by Gaertner and Dovidio (1977). Female undergraduates, tested individually, were led to believe that they were participating in an ESP experiment in which a fellow subject would attempt to send messages from another room. The subject was shown a photograph of the sender, ostensibly to establish that the two were strangers, but in fact for the purpose of varying the sender's racial identity. Also, the subject was informed either that she was the only receiver or that there were two other receivers in separate rooms. After several trials, an emergency situation was created. The sender announced over the intercom that she was going to straighten a high stack of chairs "that look as though they are about to fall." Suddenly there was a great deal of noise, and the confederate screamed that the chairs were falling on her. This was followed by prolonged silence. A helping response was scored if the subject left the sending room within a 3-minute period immediately following the occurrence of the emergency.

There was a significant interaction of the Race of Victim and Presence of Others variables, such that the black victim was helped more than the white victim when the subject believed she was alone (93.8% vs. 81.3%); whereas the direction of the difference was reversed when others were supposed to be present (37.5% vs. 75%). It would appear that white bystanders had relatively strong tendencies both to help and to avoid helping the black person, with the direction in which the conflict was resolved being determined by the presence or absence of other potential helpers. This interpretation is consistent with an assumption that subjects' racial attitudes were ambivalent. It should be noted, however, that the ambivalence-amplification model presented in Chapter 3 does not include the concept of diffusion of responsibility; hence the Gaertner and Dovidio results are not directly predictable from the model in its present form.

SUMMARY

The research presented in this chapter has dealt with a number of situational determinants of white people's overt reactions to black stimulus persons. In the field studies of Katz and associates (1975), nonwhites who displayed socially desirable attributes were treated more altruistically than whites who revealed similar qualities. Other investigators have found that the bias in favor of black help-seekers may not occur (Dovidio & Gaertner, 1977) or may even be reversed (Benson et al., 1976), when the status position pursued or occupied by the black person is relatively high. I have speculated that this withdrawal of white support tends to occur when the status sought or occupied by the minority member is perceived as inappropriate or as posing a competitive threat. In an emergency-intervention situation (Gaertner & Dovidio, 1977), the behavior of white bystanders alone or with others present suggests that they felt both more obligation to help and more aversion against helping a black accident victim than a white accident victim.

This body of research is generally consistent with an ambivalence-amplification interpretation of cross-racial behavior. However, two factors are introduced that are not explicitly included in the theoretical model: relative status of black and white interactants and presence of others. Both appear to be influential under certain conditions.

8

How Characteristics of the Handicapped Influence Helping and Other Responses of Observers

I now review evidence pertaining to the ambivalence-amplification hypothesis as it relates to interactions between physically normal subjects and handicapped individuals who reveal either positive or negative characteristics. As in the previous chapter, the main emphasis is on self-presentation and helping. But first the more general research literature on altruism and disability is reviewed.

In an early experiment on the reactions of the majority to a handicapped vis-à-vis, Kleck, Ono, and Hastorf (1966) observed that male college students talked longer with a male confederate in a wheelchair than they did with a nondisabled confederate, when they perceived that they were helping the other person perform his task as an interviewer. But the difference was in the other direction when subjects had no reason to believe that they could benefit the other by continuing to interact with him. Kleck et al. conjectured that people desire to treat the disabled kindly but find face-to-face encounters with them aversive. Data consistent with this view were reported by Doob and Ecker (1970). Suburban residents were more willing to fill out and return a questionnaire for a female door-to-door canvasser who wore an eyepatch than for one who did not, but if the request was for an interview the injured solicitor was not favored in this way. In a study by Levitt and Kornhaber (1977) involving what may be regarded as a situation of minimal social contact, both temporary and permanent disabilities elicited an increased amount of aid from strangers. Female panhandlers with either a metal leg brace and metal half-crutches or a leg cast and wooden crutches were given more money by pedestrians than were physically normal females.

However, other relevant investigations have produced little or no evidence of special kindness toward the physically impaired. Baker and Reitz (1978) had a male confederate telephone a random sample of homes and tell the person who answered that he was calling from a public booth and had dialed a wrong number with his last dime. To half of the subjects, the confederate identified himself as blind. All subjects were requested to call the correct number and leave a message. Amount of compliance was found to be only slightly greater for the blind caller than for the sighted caller. Pomazel and Clore (1973) assessed the willingness of passing motorists to assist a male or female adult who stood beside a car with a flat tire. Whether the distressed person wore a metal knee brace and an arm sling or seemed to be normal had no effect on the number of drivers who stopped to offer aid. In a study done in a shopping center by Samerotte and Harris (1976), a male confederate dropped a batch of envelopes. Passersby who saw the confederate with an eyepatch and facial scar were no more inclined to help him recover the envelopes than were people who saw him without these features. However, wearing an arm bandage did result in a higher rate of helping. Test and Bryan (1969) assigned female college students to a task that entailed some writing in a room with a same-sex peer who worked at a similar but longer task. After completing their own task, subjects were free to help the other person if they so wished. The amount of assistance actually given was the same whether the confederate's writing arm was bandaged and in a sling or uninjured—a somewhat puzzling outcome, inasmuch as temporary disability, such as would be indicated by a bandage, is not usually stigmatizing, whereas mere dependency has often been found to elicit greater helping (cf. review by Krebs, 1970).

There are also some studies in which handicapped help-seekers tended to be rejected. These studies involved types of assistance that required close contact with the recipient. Thus, in a modified replication of a part of Doob and Ecker's (1970) field experiment, Soble and Strickland (1974) had a hunchbacked or control female canvasser request housewives to participate in an interview at a future time. The canvasser informed subjects either that she would conduct the interview or that another person would do it. In the hunchback condition, substantially fewer subjects agreed to be interviewed by the confederate than agreed to be interviewed by someone else, whereas in the nonhunchback condition, a relatively high percentage of women complied regardless of whether they expected to be interviewed by the same or another person. That is, the handicapped person's solicitation tended to be refused when compliance would have entailed a future interaction with her.

Discrimination against handicapped individuals was also revealed in Pomazel and Clore's (1973) highway study. In addition to the flat tire situation already described, this investigation included a condition in which males and females posed as hitchhikers. Wearing a leg brace and arm sling was found to reduce the number of ride offers, presumably because motorists did not want to sit next to a handicapped person for any extended time. Consistent with this finding are the results of field experiments by Piliavin and associates in which a man with a cane collapsed to the floor of a subway car. Fewer onlookers gave direct assistance (involving physical contact) when the stricken person was seen to bleed from the mouth (Piliavin & Piliavin, 1972) or had a disfiguring birthmark on the face (Piliavin, Piliavin, & Rodin, 1975).

It can be seen that previous research has not revealed consistent patterns of responding to handicapped persons in need of aid. There is a suggestion in the data that the likelihood of help being given is reduced when such behavior entails face-to-face interaction with the other. But no firm conclusions can be drawn either about this factor or about other possible determinants of altruism toward the sick or injured. Not only have relatively few studies been done in this area, but the various investigators have tended to use different types of disability and different response measures, so that their findings are difficult to compare. Experiments are needed that employ similar designs and procedures to assess an array of possible determinants of prosocial behavior toward persons with bodily stigmas. One possible determinant is the attractiveness of the personal characteristics of the aid-seeker. According to the ambivalence-amplification model, the display of socially desirable or undesirable traits by handicapped individuals should tend to elicit extremely favorable or unfavorable responses from non-handicapped observers. This notion was tested empirically by Katz, Farber, Glass, Lucido, and Emswiller (1978) in a study that is described in the following paragraphs.

EXPERIMENT ON WILLINGNESS TO HELP DISABLED PERSONS WITH POSITIVE OR NEGATIVE TRAITS

Adults were administered a set of verbal tasks by a research assistant who was or was not disabled and either likeable or not likeable. Later the subjects had an opportunity to help the confederate by volunteering to be interviewed by her without pay.

Method

The subjects were 31 men and 35 women who were recruited through ads in New York City newspapers and paid for participating. They were tested in small groups with all members of a group being exposed to the same conditions. The subjects sat in chairs with writing arms, spaced far enough apart to prevent an individual from seeing what another had written. Two female graduate students served as test administrators. At each session, the tester was either seated in a wheelchair or in an ordinary chair. Cross-cutting this variable, the confederate's manner was either friendly and courteous (Positive Self-Presentation) or disinterested and caustic (Negative Self-Presentation). For example, after explaining that the purpose of the research was to pretest cognitive tasks for use in future studies, the tester mentioned in the Positive condition that she did not know much about the tasks because she was a graduate student in history and worked only part-time on the psychological testing project. In the Negative condition, she merely said that she was employed part-time on the project, adding, "So don't bother asking me any questions, because I don't really feel like answering them, even if I could." To give another example of positive and negative behavior, after handing out the test booklets the tester in the Positive condition politely requested subjects to read the instructions carefully, adding: "I realize you're not just here for the money, and I hope you'll feel you've gotten something more out of taking these tests than just that." In contrast, the following comment was made in a sullen voice in the Negative condition: "Make sure you read all the instructions very carefully, because there are always some people who manage to screw things up, no matter what. I know you're only here for the money but try to follow the directions."

The test booklet contained some mildly interesting verbal tasks such as naming as many objects with a common characteristic as one could. After 30 minutes, the research assistant collected the booklets and left the room. Shortly thereafter, a male faculty member entered and introduced himself as the project director. He told the subjects that they had just been tested in the control condition of a study that actually dealt with the effects of environmental stress on cognitive efficiency. Their test scores supposedly would provide a baseline for evaluating the performance of various experimental groups. Subjects were invited to ask questions that were answered in the context of the stress cover story, after which they were paid. Then the project director introduced the request for help, stating that the young woman who had administered the tests had asked permission, as project director, to ask a favor of the subjects. She had another part-time job, with an advertising agency, which required that she interview people about their reactions to new advertising materials. Unfortunately, she could only pay carfare money to and from her place of work. Although the real need was for interviewees, people could also help by filling out a 30-minute questionnaire that would be mailed to them with a stamped return envelope.

Subjects were given slips of paper on which to write "Not interested," "Questionnaire," or "Interview." If they wrote "Interview," they were also to indicate whether they were willing to do one, two, or three interviews. Names, addresses, and telephone numbers were also requested. Next, under the guise of following a procedure that was routine in the psychological laboratories, subjects were given a questionnaire designed to assess their anonymous impressions of the research assistant. Finally, there was a debriefing in which all deceptions were revealed.

TABLE 8.1
Means for Interaction of Disability and
Self-Presentation on Willingness to be Interviewed

| | Self-Presentation | |
Disability Status	Positive	Negative
Wheelchair	.38	1.26
Control	1.25	.53

Note: Cell *N*s range from 15 to 19.

Results

Manipulation Check.   Subjects' ratings of the test administrator provided a check on the self-presentation manipulation. A 2 × 2 × 2 analysis of variance (Tester × Self-Presentation × Handicap Status) revealed, as expected, no effects below the .10 level of significance on ratings of the tester's efficiency. But analyses of the three other items showed that in the Positive Self-Presentation condition, the tester was perceived as warmer, F (1,58) = 60.69, $p < .001$; more interested in the project, F (1,58) = 31.49, $p < .001$; and more able to motivate subjects, F (1,58) = 36.43, $p < .001$. There were no other effects for these items. Thus the manipulation of self-presentation independently of the tester and disability variables appears to have been adequate.

Compliance.   The five possible responses to the helping request were "not interested," "mail questionnaire," and "interview (one, two, or three)." The first two responses were scored 0, and the interview responses were scored 1, 2, and 3. A 2 × 2 × 2 analysis of variance of these scores yielded only one result below the .10 level of probability, an interaction effect of disability and self-presentation, F (1,58) = 9.25, $p < .01$. Cell means for the interaction are shown in Table 8.1. In the Positive condition, there was more willingness to help the nondisabled than the disabled person, t (58) = 2.30, $p < .05$; whereas in the Negative condition, it was the disabled person who received more helping commitments, t (58) = 1.89, $p = .07$.[1]

Another analysis of the compliance responses was done, using a slightly different scoring method; "mail questionnaire" was scored 1 instead of 0, and the three "interview" responses were scored 2, 3, and 4. The analysis of variance results were very similar to those obtained on the first set of scores. For the

---

[1]Because subjects were run in small groups, with all members of a group being exposed to the same experimental condition, there existed the possibility that the results were an artifact of the grouping. Therefore, the data were also analyzed with groups nested within all experimental factors. There was no effect of nested groups, F (16,42) = .10, but the interaction of Disability and Self-presentation was significant, F (1,16) = 68.97, $p < .001$, as in the prior analysis.

Disability $\times$ Self-Presentation interaction, F (1,58) = 7.56, p < .01. For the effect of disability in the Positive condition, t (58) = 1.67, p < .10; and for the effect of disability in the Negative condition, t (58) = 2.14, p < .05.

Discussion

The hypothesis was that when a nondisabled person and a disabled person had socially desirable traits subjects would respond more favorably to the disabled person, but that when both displayed socially undesirable traits, subjects would respond more favorably to the other person. What in fact occurred was diametrically opposite to the prediction. Disabled testers who were friendly and achievement-oriented were helped less than other testers with similar characteristics, whereas disabled testers who were insulting and apathetic were helped more than normal counterparts. Looking at the interaction effect another way, obnoxious behavior that in the Nondisabled condition had a detrimental effect on amount of compliance, actually had a favorable effect when the tester was disabled.

The unanticipated findings in the Positive condition cast doubt on the assumption that the personal qualities that society finds generally desirable are also the qualities that are deemed desirable in the handicapped. It appeared that a more appropriate perspective was provided by Goffman (1963) in his discussion of the stigma role that the majority group imposes upon the disabled. The latter, he argues, must know their place, keep their aspirations and achievements at a modest level, and refrain from testing the limits of the acceptance shown them. The cripple is supposed to "fulfill ordinary standards as fully as he can, stopping short only when the issue of normification arises; that is, when his efforts might give the impression that he is trying to deny his differentness [p. 115]." In a similar vein, Dembo, Leviton, and Wright (1956) maintain that members of the majority group often want the disabled to suffer as a sign that the physical assets they lack are valuable and important. Dembo et al. hypothesize that most people tend to: (1) insist that the disabled person is suffering (even when there is no evidence of suffering); or (2) devaluate the unfortunate person because he or she ought to suffer and does not.

The implication for this experiment is that subjects in the Positive Self-Presentation condition may have become angry or annoyed with the disabled confederate because she violated their beliefs about how people confined to wheelchairs are supposed to behave. That is, instead of seeming to feel inadequate, she was outgoing, competent, and achievement-oriented. This could account for the relatively small amount of helping that occurred in the Disabled–Positive condition. The stigma–role conception of Goffman and Dembo et al. can also account for the reversal of the disability effect in the Negative condition, in which the handicapped tester's rudeness and apathy could have been seen by subjects as a consequence of misfortune, causing them to feel sorry for her and treat her kindly. In contrast, the control confederate's obnoxious behavior, being taken at face value, led to angry rejection of the helping request. If these conjectures are correct, covert anger should have been relatively high in the Disabled–Positive and Control–Negative conditions, as compared with Control–Positive and Disabled–Negative conditions. Also, the tester should have been perceived as less happy in the Disabled–Negative condition than in any of the other conditions. To test these conjectures, another experiment was done.

EXPERIMENT ON ANGER

Subjects were exposed to the same manipulations as were used in the first experiment, following which covert anger and perception of the tester's mood state were assessed. The measure of anger was a paper-and-pencil test that required subjects to generate synonyms for several stimulus words, including the word "anger." The notion was that the higher the subject's internal state of anger arousal, the more anger-related responses would be cued off by the "anger" label. In addition to "anger," other hostile stimulus words were included in the synonyms test to explore possible generalization effects. Also, neutral words were included as control stimuli. To measure the subject's perception of the confederate as relatively happy or unhappy, two 9-point scales were added to the impression-rating questionnaire: "cheerful–uncheerful" and "at ease and relaxed–tense and anxious."

Method

A sample of 29 men and 38 women were recruited through local newspaper ads and paid to participate in the study. The part of the experimental procedure involving the confederate was similar to that of the first experiment, except that: (1) a male graduate student enacted the role of test administrator in all conditions; and (2) subjects were given two new tests instead of the ones used previously—a brief filler task and the synonyms test.

The synonyms test consisted of five aggression words from the Buss (1961) list, selected to represent different levels of intensity of hostility. The key word was "anger," which had about median Buss intensity values for males and females respectively, and a relatively high Lorge–Thorndike frequency count. The four additional words that were selected from the top quartile of intensity values were "harm," "fight," "hatred," and "murder." There were also eight neutral words: "large," "build," "end," "quick," "teach," "heavy," "show," and "communicate." The aggression words were scattered throughout the list, with "anger" appearing as the seventh item. Subjects were given a test booklet filled with blank pages and instructed on each trial to write a particular stimulus word at the top of a new page, and then to write under it as many words of similar meaning as time allowed. Each trial lasted 90 seconds and was followed by a 20-second rest period.

As in the first experiment, when the tests had been completed the confederate left the room, and the "project director" appeared to administer a postexperimental questionnaire and debrief the subjects. None of them expressed suspicion of experimental deception.

Results

Manipulation Check. There were no effects on ratings of the tester's efficiency. But analyses of ratings of warmth, interest in project, and ability to motivate subjects showed that scores on each were more favorable in the Positive condition than in the Negative condition ($ps < .001$). There were no other effects for these items. Thus the manipulation of self-presentation appears to have been adequate.

Responses on Synonyms Test. Regarding number of responses to the stimulus word "anger," the only significant effect was an interaction of Disability Status and Self-Presentation, $F (1,63) = 5.25$, $p = .02$. As shown in Table 8.2, the pattern of cell means conforms to the experimental prediction. That is, in the Positive Self-Presentation condition, the disabled tester occasioned more anger responses than the nondisabled one; whereas in the Negative Self-Presentation condition, the difference was in the opposite direction. The difference was significant in the Positive condition, $t (63) = 2.34$, $p < .05$, but not in the Negative condition.[2]

Responses to the four other hostile stimulus words were analyzed separately and also in combination, but there were no effects. Similarly, no effects were obtained when responses to the eight neutral stimulus words were analyzed separately or in combination.

Perception of Suffering. The impression questionnaire included two items dealing with subjects' perceptions of the confederate's affective state. On each item, the only finding was a main effect of self-presentation. In the Negative condition, as compared with the Positive condition, the tester was seen as less cheerful ($Ms = 3.21$ and 6.87), $F (1,63) = 114.57$, $p < .001$, and more anxious ($Ms = 4.61$ and 2.30), $F (1,63) = 40.83$, $p < .001$.

---

[2]Because subjects were run in small groups, with all members of a group being exposed to the same experimental condition, the data were also analyzed with groups nested within all experimental factors. There was no effect of nested groups, $F (16,47) = .14$, but the interaction of Disability and Self-presentation was significant, $F (1,16) = 29.23$, $p > .001$, as in the prior analysis.

TABLE 8.2
Mean Number of "Anger" Responses in
Each Experiment Treatment

Disability Status	Self-Presentation	
	Positive	Negative
Wheelchair	6.41	5.50
Nonwheelchair	4.88	6.12

Note: $N = 16$ in the Wheelchair–Negative cell and 17 in all other cells.

DISCUSSION

Summarizing the results of both experiments as regards compliance and anger, wheelchair-bound confederates who displayed positive characteristics were helped less and occasioned more covert anger than nondisabled counterparts, whereas the former were treated more kindly and occasioned somewhat less anger than the latter when both displayed negative characteristics. These results appear to contradict the prediction derived from the ambivalence-amplification model. A plausible interpretation of the discrepancy is that the investigators failed to recognize that behaviors and personality traits ordinarily deemed desirable in most people may not be considered desirable in the physically disabled. By employing the stigma notions of Dembo et al. and Goffman to account for the data on compliance in the first experiment, it was possible to predict with some success the results later obtained on responsiveness to an anger cue.

In the second experiment, responses to the stimulus word "anger" showed the predicted effects, whereas there were no effects on responses to the hostile words "hatred," "fight," "harm," and "murder." It would seem that "anger" was the only verbal cue that described the feeling state presumed to be aroused in the Wheelchair–Positive and Control–Negative conditions. That is, the observations of Dembo et al. (1956) and Goffman (1963) suggested that subjects would be angered when the handicapped person in the Positive condition violated the stigma–role requirements of suffering and acknowledged inadequacy. In addition, common sense indicated that resentment would be aroused when the other confederate in the Negative condition behaved obnoxiously. Of the five hostile words, only "anger" and "hatred" refer to feeling states per se, and of the two, the latter would seem to denote too extreme an emotion to have been a suitable affective cue. As for "fight," "murder," and "harm," these words, which denote active aggression, were probably too extreme in their hostile implications, or too anxiety-arousing, to elicit a high level of responding.

In the Wheelchair–Negative condition, the confederate's self-presentation as a caustic, apathetic individual with ambiguous goals presumably was not inconsistent with the stigma–role prescription that Dembo et al, and Goffman describe. It

was expected that subjects would perceive the disabled person's negative behavior as a sign of suffering. But only partly in keeping with the prediction was
the finding that *both* the disabled and the nondisabled tester were seen as less
cheerful and more anxious in the Negative condition than in the Positive one.
However, it is perhaps not unreasonable to assume that in the Wheelchair–
Negative condition, subjects tended to ascribe the tester's apparent unhappiness,
at least in part, to his disability, and therefore to feel sorry for him.

Admittedly, the results presented in this chapter were not anticipated and are
not supportive of the ambivalence model. Additional experiments are needed to
explore the specific elements in the confederate's behavior that caused the intended Positive Self-Presentation condition to produce an effect opposite to the
initial prediction. The explanation I have offered is not a compelling one, but at
present there appear to be no plausible alternatives.

9

Forming Impressions of Stigmatized Persons with Positive or Negative Traits

Further investigations of reactions to stigmatized strangers who reveal positive or negative characteristics are now presented. In all of the studies in this chapter, subjects' responses consist of impression ratings and other verbal measures of liking and acceptance. The hypothesis to which they are relevant parallels the hypothesis of the previous chapter: stigmatized persons will be evaluated more positively than nonstigmatized persons when both display socially desirable qualities, and more negatively when both display socially undesirable qualities. There have been several experiments of this kind that employed black or disabled individuals as targets.

DIENSTBIER'S EXPERIMENTS

Dienstbier (1970) had 80 white male high school students in the North read and evaluate two personality profiles, one of which was black, one white. One of the profiles pertained to a person who had beliefs and values of high social desirability; the other profile described an individual with characteristics generally low in social desirability. Subjects who were presented the desirable profile as that of a white person evaluated the undesirable profile as that of a black; other subjects received the opposite stimulus combinations.

The favorable sketch depicted a likable and socially successful male high school junior who was college bound upon his graduation, and whose ideas were "a lot like those of most people his age." The unfavorable sketch described a male 17-year-old high school dropout who was a somewhat greedy, shy, and rebellious social misfit.

The evaluation questionnaire consisted of scales for reporting liking and acceptance of the stimulus person.

There was found to be a tendency in the Positive Sketch condition, apparent on 15 out of 19 scales, for subjects to react more favorably to the black than to the white target person. But the negative profile elicited differences in the opposite direction, with the white target being evaluated more highly on 16 of the 19 measures. However, for only three of the items was the interaction of race and type of sketch significant at the .05 level. The items were perceived similarity between self and stimulus person, willingness to accept him as an intimate friend, and willingness to elect him to political office. That is, although ratings in the Positive and Negative conditions were consistently more extreme when the person being evaluated was black as compared with white, most of the differences were quite small.

Seeking to confirm what he referred to as a "positive prejudice" phenomenon in the Positive Profile condition, Dienstbier did a second experiment that was similar to the first one, except that two sketches of college girls were used, both of which emphasized socially desirable traits, and the subjects were University of Rochester female undergraduates. Differences in favor of the black stimulus persons were apparent on 13 of the 19 scales, and seven of these differences were statistically significant. Thus the "positive prejudice" finding of the first study was convincingly replicated.

Altogether, Dienstbier's work provided: (1) moderate support for the response-amplification prediction; and (2) stronger evidence of a pro-black tendency when target persons of both races were depicted favorably. But these effects were revealed only on scales that dealt with liking and respect, or acceptance in relatively informal, voluntary relationships that could be terminated fairly readily. When the hypothetical association was more formal or permanent, the minority members were consistently rejected. In both experiments there were strong main effects indicative of anti-black bias ($ps < .01$) on the following three attitude items: would exclude from own neighborhood, would accept as a close kin through marriage, would accept as next door neighbor. It would seem, then, that the distinction between behaviors that entail binding recognition versus those that do not is an important one. But this distinction has not been pursued by subsequent investigators who have used research designs similar to Dienstbier's.

THE UNIVERSITY OF TEXAS STUDIES

Attempted Replication of Dienstbier

Carver, Glass, Snyder, and Katz (1977) set out to replicate Dienstbier's response-amplification finding with a sample of male sophomores at the University of Texas. The 106 subjects had previously been administered a short version of the Woodmansee and Cook (1967) racial prejudice scale and Schuman and Harding's (1963) scale on sympathetic identification with the ethnic underdog. Each man read a two-page transcript of a fictitious interview, ostensibly as part of a study on impression formation. In the Nonstigmatized condition, a line across the top of both pages read "Dan B., Male, 19, 5'9", 150 pounds." In the Black condition, the word "Black" was added to the description. The two transcripts were otherwise identical within each of two favorability conditions. The favorable transcript portrayed the interviewee as a college student with an upper-middle-class background, high ambitions, varied interests, and many friends. The unfavorable transcript portrayed the interviewee as a college student from a lower-class background, with few friends, no particular interests, and no plans for the future. Each subject evaluated one interviewee by means of a 20-item questionnaire consisting of five trait clusters—likability, warmth, conceit, intelligence, and adjustment.

In addition to a favorability main effect, $F (1,102) = 60.71$, $p < .001$, there was a nonsignificant tendency for blacks to be rated more positively than whites across both transcript conditions, $F (1,102) = 2.71$, $p < .10$. The mean ratings for each of the four stigma by transcript conditions are presented in Table 9.1. It can be seen that the race difference for the Negative Transcript condition went counter to the amplification prediction and to Dienstbier's results.

The only suggestion of support for the amplification prediction in the Negative Transcript condition came from a comparison of subjects' racial attitude scores with their evaluations of the black stimulus person. Men who scored above the median on both the racial prejudice and racial sympathy scales (i.e., relatively ambivalent subjects) rated the negatively portrayed black less favorably than did subjects with any of the three other combinations of high or low prejudice and high or low sympathy scores ($ps < .05$).

Carver and his associates did three replications of the foregoing experiment, with procedural modifications. In Experiment II, 73 male students were subjected to the same procedure as had been used previously, except that

TABLE 9.1
Mean Impression Ratings Under
Four Stigma by Favorability Conditions[a]

Experiment	Positive Transcript		Negative Transcript	
	Stigma	Nonstigma	Stigma	Nonstigma
I	29.69	27.69	6.26	−3.21
II	90.90	86.93	83.11	68.95
III	36.48	28.85	−6.15	−17.50
IV	27.10	24.14	−11.45	−14.26

Note: Stimulus persons were black in Experiments I through III, and Chicano in Experiment IV. In each case, more positive numbers indicate higher evaluations.

[a] Adapted from Carver et al. (1977).

Dienstbier's rating scales were used to assess reactions to the stimulus person. Also, in this experiment as well as the later ones, measures of general racial attitudes were not taken. The only relevant finding in Experiment II was a main effect for race, F (1,69) = 7.47, p < .01. As shown in Table 9.1, subjects evaluated the black stimulus person more favorably than the white across both transcript conditions, thereby reproducing the outcome of the first experiment.

Experiment III tested the possibility that the discrepancy between the Texas findings and those of Dienstbier was due to a change in the status of the negatively depicted stimulus person from high school dropout to college student. One hundred and seven male students were tested according to the procedures of Experiment I, except that the interview transcripts were altered to portray boys of high school age, one clearly bound for college and success, the other a dropout. The relevant finding—a main effect of race, F (1,103) = 7.37, p < .01— duplicated the results of Experiments I and II (see Table 9.1).

Experiment IV was done to determine whether the bias shown by subjects in favor of black target persons would be evident toward members of another ethnic minority group, Chicanos. The procedure used in the previous experiment was applied to a sample of 109 male undergraduates, except that the transcript identification was changed from black to Chicano. The data revealed no effects involving ethnicity. As can be seen in Table 9.1, the pattern of treatment means was in the direction of a pro-minority effect, but the differences were very small. Apparently, Texas undergraduates are less aware of Chicanos than of blacks as a disadvantaged minority group.

Summarizing, in three studies Carver et al. failed to replicate Dienstbier's finding of both positive and negative response amplification toward black stimulus persons. Instead, they found that identifying an anonymous other as black had a favorable effect on subjects' evaluations of him, regardless of the nature of the personal characteristics he displayed. It is possible that the discrepancy in results was connected to the sampling difference. Dienstbier's subjects were high school juniors, whereas the Texas investigators used college students. The latter, being older and therefore more attuned to prevailing social norms, may have been more concerned about gaining the experimenter's approval by expressing a tolerant racial attitude. Or, being better informed about civil rights issues, the college sample may have perceived the black stimulus person as having overcome special environmental barriers to success and credited him for this (a possibility that accords with Kelley's, 1971, attributional principle of "augmentation"). Research addressed to these issues is presented later in this chapter, but I first consider an experiment on reactions to the handicapped.

Evaluations of Handicapped Individuals

The purpose of this study by Scheier, Carver, Schulz, Glass, and Katz (1978) was to see whether the favorableness that marked evaluations of black targets in the foregoing experiments of Carver and others would also be observed toward the handicapped. A second aim was to assess the effect on these ratings of self-focused attention. The investigators reasoned that if high ratings of handicapped persons were a reflection of an arousal of sympathy, then the most positive ratings should be given by those subjects who were most aware of their sympathy. A perceiver who was self-aware should be more cognizant of his affective response than one who was not self-aware, hence should evaluate the handicapped target more positively when his attention was self-focused than when it was directed outward.

The subjects, 160 male and female students at the University of Texas, were administered a questionnaire constructed by Fenigstein, Scheier, and Buss (1975), which purportedly measures individual differences in private self-consciousness, or the disposition to be aware of one's inner thoughts, feelings, and motives. High and low private self-consciousness groups were determined by a median split, and within levels of self-consciousness, subjects were randomly assigned to one of four conditions at another session. The conditions were positive or negative interview and handicapped or nonhandicapped target. The experimental procedure was similar to that of the earlier Texas studies, except that the interviewee was described as a male undergraduate who was either physically handicapped (a paraplegic confined to a wheelchair) or not, and subjects rated the interviewee on 11 descriptive dimensions (e.g., intelligent–unintelligent, hardworking–lazy).

Analysis of subjects' summed ratings yielded two significant findings involving the handicap variable. First, as anticipated by the investigators, there was a main effect in which the paraplegic was rated more favorably than the nonhandicapped person, $F (1,152) = 8.61$, $p < .01$. Also as predicted, there was in interaction of self-consciousness and target, $F (1,152) = 4.85$, $p < .03$, which indicated that private self-consciousness enhanced the tendency for the stigmatized person to be evaluated more positively than the other person, $t (152) = 2.44$, $p < .02$, whereas the two self-consciousness groups did not differ in their ratings of the nonstigmatized target, $t < 1.0$.

Interestingly, another type of score derivable from the self-consciousness questionnaire—*public* self-consciousness, or awareness of self as a social object that is responded to by others—showed no relationship to the impression ratings. It appears, then, that the favorable evaluations of the paraplegic were not motivated by a desire to behave in a socially approved manner. If social conformity had been the motive, the stigmatized target should have been rated most positively by those subjects who were most sensitive to their public image, i.e., who were high in public self-consciousness. On the other hand, the results for *private* self-consciousness suggest that the favorable evaluations of the paraplegic were an expression of positive feelings such as sympathy that were aroused by the disability cues in the interview transcripts. However, this does not rule out the possibility that aversive reactions to the paraplegic also occurred—reactions that were unconsciously denied, hence not available for scrutiny even when the perceiver's attention was directed inward.

The Bogus Pipeline Study

To learn more about factors underlying the majority group's tendency to show a high level of approval of black and handicapped interviewees in the Negative Transcript condition of the preceding experiments, Carver, Glass, and Katz (1978) decided to employ Jones and Sigall's (1971) "bogus pipeline" technique of attitude measurement. This approach involves convincing the subject that the experimenter can monitor his true emotional reactions to any stimulus by means of elaborate physiological recording apparatus. The subject's task supposedly is to guess accurately his own affective responses as revealed on an electronic meter. Sigall and Page (1971) have presented data from several studies that seem to show that the bogus pipeline setup elicits higher prejudice scores from subjects than are obtained under control conditions.

Ninety female undergraduates at the University of Texas participated in the experiment, which they were told initially dealt with impression formation. They all read the negative interview transcript that had been used by Carver et al. (1977) in Experiments I, II, and IV. That is, the stimulus person was depicted as a male college student from a lower-class background who had few friends, no particular interests, and no plans for the future. Subjects were randomly assigned to either a Bogus Pipeline or No Pipeline condition, and to three stigma conditions in which the interviewee was identified as either black, physically handicapped (a paraplegic confined to a wheelchair), or nonstigmatized.

In the No Pipeline condition, subjects read the transcript and then rated the stimulus person on 11 evaluative trait dimensions (e.g., intelligent–unintelligent, hardworking–lazy). In the Bogus condition, electrodes from an elaborate piece of electronic apparatus were attached to the subject, who was told that the equipment could not only measure the strength of emotional reactions to another person but could also distinguish whether the reactions were positive or negative. After reading the interview transcript, the subject was instructed to estimate her GSR response to each of the 11 trait dimensions by marking a point on a scale. As the scales used in the Bogus condition were the same as those used in the No Pipeline condition, the summed ratings for the two conditions were comparable.

Analysis of the evaluation scores (see Fig. 9.1) yielded a significant interaction of the pipeline and stigma variables, F (2,84) = 3.65, $p < .03$, such that the bogus pipeline manipulation had an impact on subjects' ratings only when the stimulus person was labeled as black. Subsequent contrasts indicated that subjects rated the black interviewee significantly more negatively in the Pipeline condition than in the No Pipeline condition, t (84) = 2.86, $p < .01$, but the ratings did not differ between these two conditions for either the handicapped or the nonstigmatized interviewee, ts < 1.

Subjects overall rated the handicapped interviewee more favorably than they rated the nonstigmatized interviewee, t (84) = 2.16, $p < .05$. In line with the earlier findings of Carver et al. (1977), control subjects tended to rate the black above the nonstigmatized interviewee, t (84) = 1.92, $p < .06$. This tendency

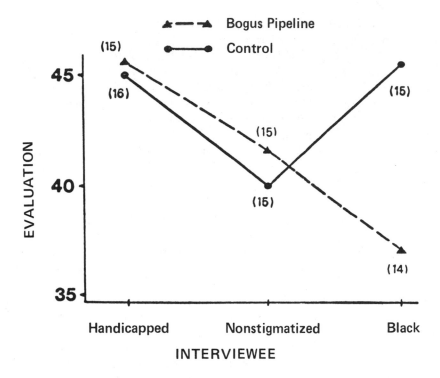

FIG. 9.1.   Evaluations of unfavorably portrayed stimulus persons: impression ratings versus bogus pipeline (a larger number indicates a more favorable evaluation; group Ns in parentheses).

was reversed in the Pipeline condition, but the difference between those means was not statistically reliable, t (84) = 1.53, $p < .13$.

The data suggest that subjects in the No Pipeline condition were to some extent aware of having strongly negative reactions to the black stimulus person but tried to disguise these reactions in order to demonstrate either to themselves or to the experimenter that they were unprejudiced. Presumably, the pipeline instructions caused them to reveal their actual feelings. The lower ratings assigned to the black rather than to the nonhandicapped white person by subjects on the pipeline are consistent with Dienstbier's finding and with the prediction from the ambivalence model of amplified negative responsivity to blacks displaying socially undesirable characteristics. Recall that the earlier interview transcript studies, which did not employ the bogus pipeline, produced results consistent with the ambivalence hypothesis for the Favorable Transcript condition only. That is, in that condition, subjects reacted more positively to the black than to the white person (as in Dienstbier's experiment).

The pipeline manipulation had no effect on evaluations of the paraplegic, which were higher than the evaluations of the nonstigmatized interviewee overall. It is not really clear why ratings of the handicapped person were unaffected by the pipeline procedure. One possibility, of course, is that subjects were actually very favorably disposed toward him. But in line with my earlier discussion of the self-consciousness study, it may be that derogatory thoughts about one who is physically disabled are more stringently denied by most people than are comparable sentiments about a black. The bogus pipeline condition may simply not have been strong enough to break through subjects' unconscious defenses against recognizing their aversive reactions.[1]

RESEARCH BY LINVILLE AND JONES

In an innovative approach to the investigation of cross-racial impression formation, Linville and Jones (1980) sought to correct two apparent weaknesses of most previous questionnaire studies in this area: their relatively noninvolving nature and the ostensible lack of privacy of one's responses. Linville and Jones had college students evaluate fictitious applications to an Ivy League law school, using instructions that stressed three points: (1) that their evaluations would have no conceivable consequences for the particular applicants; (2) that their ratings were completely anonymous; and (3) that the results of the study, presumably sponsored by the "National Law School Association," would provide a basis for decisions regarding policies and methods in the selection of law students.

The subjects, 192 white male and female undergraduates at Duke University, were told that the specific goal of the research was to discover which portions of a law school application were the most diagnostic of a student's future performance in law school. Each subject was given a booklet containing portions of three applications that provided incidental information about the applicant's sex and race. The first two applications (a white male and a white female) were fillers to disguise the purpose of the study and were identical for all subjects. The third application contained crucial information regarding the applicant's sex and race. Presumably submitted by a student accepted to law school, it included the applicant's college honors and activities. There was also a faculty evaluation and an essay written by the applicant describing why he or she wanted to study law. High versus low favorability of the applicant's credentials was manipulated by varying scholastic honors and activities, the articulateness of the essay, and the

---

[1]Another possibility that might be considered distinguishes between true feelings and what the subject suspects might be his true feelings. If one assumes that people are generally aware that prejudice toward blacks exists and is widespread, but not so aware that prejudice toward people in wheelchairs exists, then it might be conjectured that subjects would be more willing to acknowledge having some prejudice toward blacks than the same amount of prejudice toward the handicapped.

strength of the faculty evaluation. The strong application was truly outstanding, whereas the weak application was of marginal quality for admission to a prestigious law school.

The independent variables, then, were race, sex, and favorability of the application, with an equal number of subjects being randomly assigned to each combination of conditions.

After reading each application, the subject rated the applicant on 15 bipolar adjectives reflecting traits relevant to law school performance. Statistical analysis showed no significant main effects for race on ratings of individual items. The interactions of race and strength of application are shown in Table 9.2. Although the number of significant findings is not high, the consistency of the interactive pattern is striking. When the applicant information was strongly positive, the black applicant was rated more highly than the white applicant on 14 of the 15 traits. When the application was weak, the black applicant was rated more negatively than the white applicant on 11 out of 15 items. The specific traits showing significant Race $\times$ Strength interactions were intelligent, creative in thought, persistent, and likable. Summed ratings for the 15 scales (overall favorability) yielded a marginally significant interaction, $p < .10$.

TABLE 9.2
Mean Ratings of Trait Items as a Function of
Strength of Application and Race of Applicant[a]

	Condition				
Measure	Pos. White	Pos. Black	Neg. White	Neg. Black	Strength $\times$ Race F (1,176)
Creative in thought	24.73	29.75	19.71	19.08	6.17***
Good writer	28.67	30.17	12.83	14.08	.01
Intelligent	28.19	29.71	16.98	14.96	4.43**
Articulate speaker	28.63	30.92	18.60	17.75	2.48
Logical and analytical	28.79	29.67	20.04	19.48	.62
Astute judgment	29.60	31.10	24.04	23.71	1.38
Hard-working	33.40	33.92	24.35	23.90	.35
Persistent	30.33	31.71	24.04	21.29	4.53**
Motivated	31.60	33.83	24.23	24.52	.95
Dedicated	31.73	33.27	22.83	22.29	1.20
Aggressive	27.90	26.69	20.23	19.56	.07
Takes initiative	27.19	28.19	21.77	20.69	1.47
Resourceful	28.94	30.54	21.81	22.06	.48
Leader	28.27	30.27	19.02	20.60	.04
Likable	28.58	31.96	30.15	29.71	4.85**
Overall favorability	29.10	30.78	21.38	20.91	2.90*

Note: High scores indicate more of the trait or factor designated.
[a]Adapted from Linville and Jones (1980).
*p < .10.   **p < .05.   ***p < .01.

The results, though not as strong as one would wish, generally support the response-amplification hypothesis. They are similar to Dienstbier's (1970) findings for comparable evaluative items but are at variance with the Texas data. The latter, it will be recalled, revealed favoring of black interviewees in both the Positive and Negative Transcript conditions (except when the bogus pipeline was used), a bias that perhaps reflected subjects' unwillingness to reveal critical racial attitudes. Linville and Jones tried to increase the candor of subjects' responses by stressing anonymity and the important use to which the evaluations would be put. Apparently the strategy worked.

Linville and Jones believe that their results reflect a polarization phenomenon common to situations in which observers receive new information about members of an outgroup. Their view is that people's cognitive schemas regarding outgroup members tend to be relatively simplified and undifferentiated, so that new information can more heavily influence one's impression of a stranger if he is an outgroup member than if he is an ingroup member. Linville and Jones' formulation is discussed more fully in Chapter 10.

ADDITIONAL STUDIES OF REACTIONS
TO THE HANDICAPPED

I return now to the work of Carver and others on adult subjects' evaluations of stimulus persons identified as physically handicapped. In two additional studies, there were attempts to improve upon the procedures used in the earlier interview transcript experiments in order to demonstrate amplification of both positive and negative responses to disabled individuals.

Experimental Arousal of Ambivalence

The authors of the first investigation (Carver, Gibbons, Stephan, Glass, & Katz, 1979) point out that in the earlier experiments by Carver et al. (1978) and Scheier at al. (1978), ambivalence about handicapped people in general may not have been salient. If subjects' did not experience attitudinal conflict in the experimental situation, there would be no reason to expect response amplification to occur. Therefore, a procedure was devised for arousing subjects' ambivalent attitudes toward the disabled just prior to their being shown the interview transcripts.

Method.   Subjects in this experiment were 248 female undergraduates at the University of Texas. Half were exposed to a pretreatment intended to increase the salience of both sympathetic and aversive feelings toward the handicapped, and the other half were not. Then, as in the earlier experiments, subjects read positive or negative interview transcripts and evaluated the interviewees. It was expected that subjects whose ambivalence was experimentally heightened would show positive and negative response amplification, whereas control subjects would not.

A male confederate posing as a student approached the subject while she waited in the hall for the experiment to begin. He told her that he was circulating a petition to the Student-Faculty Senate, calling for a campus-wide referendum on the enrollment of disabled students. The cover page of the petition presented arguments both for and against having lower admission standards for physically disabled applicants than for nondisabled ones. The ostensible purpose of the message was to inform students of the issues involved, but the actual intention was to arouse conflicting feelings and beliefs about people with disabilities.

The statement in support of increased admissions for the handicapped admonished the student populace for avoiding "uncomfortable" questions involving the rights of handicapped people. It pointed out that this group faced barriers to equal educational and economic opportunities. The intent was to evoke feelings of sympathy for them. The next paragraph presented an opposing argument, citing the likelihood that a sudden increase in the enrollment of handicapped students would cause admission to be denied to more qualified students. Mentioned also was the fact that funds would have to be diverted from other important projects to build additional special facilities for disabled persons. Here the intent was to evoke negative affect toward the handicapped. In conclusion, it was stressed that support existed for each position in the senate and that students should be fully informed on the issues involved.

After reading the cover sheet, subjects were asked to sign a petition requesting that students be allowed to voice their opinions in a referendum. The experimenter then appeared and escorted the subject to an experimental cubicle, where she read a transcript of an interview with a male undergraduate who had either socially desirable or undesirable attributes. (The transcripts were the same as those used by Carver et al., 1977, to depict college students.) In addition, the interviewee was either handicapped (paraplegic and confined to a wheelchair), Chicano, or nonstigmatized. The Chicano transcripts were included to test the notion that experimentally induced ambivalence toward one stigmatized group may generalize to another stigmatized group.

After reading the transcript, the subject evaluated the interviewee on a series of bipolar trait scales (e.g., intelligent–unintelligent, and hardworking–lazy). The ratings were summed to yield an overall score.

Results.   Group means for the evaluation scores are presented in Table 9.3. Analysis revealed that the favorably presented interviewees were rated more positively than the unfavorably presented ones, $p < .001$. More importantly, there was a highly significant favorability by pretreatment interaction, $F(1,236) = 17.77$, $p < .001$, such that the favorably portrayed interviewees were rated more positively following pretreatment than with no pretreatment, $t(236) = 3.84$, $p < .001$; and the unfavorably portrayed interviewees were rated more negatively following pretreatment than with no pretreatment, $t(236) = 2.08$, $p < .04$.

TABLE 9.3
Mean Evaluations of the Interviewees[a]

| | Favorable Portrayal | | Unfavorable Portrayal | |
	Pretreatment	Control	Pretreatment	Control
Handicapped	104.47	99.20	64.90	71.39
Chicano	101.33	88.10	59.95	64.29
Nonstigmatized	101.61	93.95	57.00	58.96

Note: Higher numbers indicate more positive evaluations.
[a] Adapted from Carver et al. (1979).

To determine the generality of the amplification effect, the strength of the favorability by pretreatment interaction was examined separately for each stimulus group. The interaction proved to be significant for interviewees labeled as handicapped ($p < .04$) and for those labeled as Chicano ($p < .01$) and to be marginally significant for those who were unlabeled ($p < .08$).

The overall analysis also revealed a significant main effect for stimulus group, $F (2,236) = 8.98$, $p < .001$, reflecting the fact that handicapped interviewees were rated more positively overall than either Chicanos or the nonstigmatized. Ratings of the latter groups did not differ reliably from each other. These findings replicated results obtained earlier by Carver et al. (1978) and Scheier et al. (1978).

Discussion. The main purpose of the experiment had been to demonstrate that when ambivalence against handicapped peers in general was made salient, college students would make more extreme evaluations of disabled individuals than of nonstigmatized targets. This purpose was not realized. Although evaluations of the paraplegic interviewees were more extreme in the Pretreatment condition, this effect generalized to other targets—to Chicanos and even somewhat to nonstigmatized persons. Polarization of responses was no more pronounced toward the handicapped targets than toward the Chicano or nonstigmatized targets.

The generalization of the pretreatment effect in the present study may have been caused by the presence of arousal. That is, by making attitudinal conflict toward the handicapped more salient, the pretreatment may have increased the subject's level of drive, or excitation, thereby causing all prepotent responses to be expressed more fully. Alternatively, as attribution theory would suggest, it may be that arousal became dissociated from its initial source due to the change in context (cf. Zillmann, Johnson, & Day, 1974). That is, as the subject read the interview transcript, she may have attributed her arousal to the content of the interview. In Chapter 10, both arousal conceptions are discussed more fully in comparison with the ambivalence-amplification model.

Amplified Responses to a Disabled Partner

Gibbons, Stephan, Stephenson, and Petty (in press) conjectured that the interview setup used in previous studies of reactions to handicapped stimulus persons was not sufficiently involving to elicit strong expressions of affect. Their first two experiments demonstrated that the positivity effect obtained in the interview transcript studies (i.e., higher evaluations of a disabled person than of a nondisabled one in both the favorable and unfavorable self-presentation conditions) could be replicated even when subjects witnessed a live interview or a videotape of an interview. They concluded that the interview format was not involving enough to produce response amplification, even when the stimulus person was more salient. In the next experiment, Gibbons et al. placed subjects in a situation of face-to-face interaction with a disabled actor, where the confederate's behavior supposedly had pleasant or unpleasant consequences for the subject. With this procedure, amplification of both positive and negative responses toward the stigmatized other was successfully demonstrated.

Each of 60 female undergraduates was matched with a female confederate who posed as either a disabled or nondisabled fellow subject. (In the former condition, the confederate walked with the assistance of metal hand-grip crutches and mentioned to the experimenter that she had a permanent hip injury.) The experimenter explained to the dyad that each person would be given eight anagrams to solve and that their combined score would be compared with the scores of other dyads. The difficulty of the anagrams was manipulated so that the subject always got three or four correct while the confederate got either none or seven correct. When both partners had completed their trials, they were told that their total score, relative to that of other teams, was either high (Success condition) or low (Failure condition), an outcome for which the confederate clearly was primarily responsible. Next, the two women were separated, and the subject filled out a questionnaire that included a set of 12 bipolar trait scales for evaluating the partner. The trait ratings were summed to yield an overall score.

In accordance with the response-amplification prediction, there was a strong interaction effect of the handicap and outcome variables on the trait ratings, $F(1,156) = 12.18$, $p < .001$ (see Table 9.4). Subjects who received success

TABLE 9.4
Means for Interaction of Handicap
and Outcome on Total Ratings of Confederate[a]

	Success	*Failure*
Handicapped partner	96.47	48.27
Nonhandicapped partner	84.31	58.00

Note: High numbers indicate more favorable evaluation.

[a] From Gibbons et al. (in press).

feedback with a handicapped partner evaluated her more positively than did those who succeeded with a nonhandicapped partner, t (56) = 3.25, p < .01. In contrast, when subjects failed in the Handicapped condition, they tended to evaluate the partner more negatively than they did when they failed in the Nonhandicapped condition, t (56) = 1.93, p < .07. There was also a substantial main effect of success–failure, with evaluations being more favorable in the Success condition, F (1,56) = 138.16, p < .001, but the handicap main effect was nonsignificant.

In looking at the results of this experiment, it is not clear whether the amplification effect occurred because: (1) the partner was shown to have high or low mental ability; or (2) the partner was responsible for the subject's experience of success or failure. These two factors were confounded in the manipulation of the outcome variable. To clarify this issue, another experiment was done by Gibbons et al. in which the relevance of a male partner's behavior and his level of performance were varied independently. The general procedure was similar to that of the prior experiment with two major exceptions: The confederate was always handicapped; and in one condition (High Relevance) he worked together with the subject as a teammate on the anagram task, whereas in a second condition (Low Relevance) he worked independently. The subjects were male undergraduates. In the Low Relevance condition, the true subject and the confederate were told that they would be working independently and that the scores of each would be compared separately with those of other students; in the High Relevance condition, they were told that they would be working independently on their anagrams, but when they were finished, their individual scores would be combined to form a single team score, which would be compared with the scores of other dyads. The difficulty of the anagrams was manipulated so that the subject always got four correct and the confederate got either one or seven correct, which meant a team total that was either high or low relative to other dyads in the High Relevance condition.

As in the previous experiment, the confederate received more favorable evaluations when he performed well than when he performed poorly, F (1,46) = 21.09, p < .001 (see Table 9.5). In addition, the anticipated interaction between

TABLE 9.5
Means for Interaction of Relevance and
Partner's Ability on Total Ratings of Him[a]

	High Relevance		Low Relevance	
High performance	99.92	(12)	84.58	(13)
Low performance	69.77	(12)	78.46	(13)

Note: Numbers in parentheses are cell Ns. High numbers indicate more favorable evaluation.

[a] Adapted from Gibbons et al. (in press).

relevance and performance was significant, F (1,46) = 9.25, $p < .004$. The predicted amplification effect was obtained in that the successful, relevant person received higher ratings, F (1,46) = 7.24, $p < .01$, whereas the unsuccessful, relevant person tended to receive lower ratings, F (1,46) = 2.50, $p = .12$, than the comparable Low Relevance person. Finally, the simple effect of performance was significant in the High Relevance condition, F (1,46) = 29.16, but not in the Low Relevance condition. F (1,46) = 1.21, $p < .20$.

These findings would seem to indicate that it is only when the confederate is responsible for team success or failure that the subject's evaluations of him are extremely favorable or unfavorable. However, another interpretation can be drawn. It seems reasonable that in the independent (Low Relevance) situation, the subject would have tended to see the confederate as a competitor whose score on the anagrams task was better or worse than his own, so that when the confederate performed well the subject would experience failure, and when the confederate performed poorly he would experience success. But in the team (High Relevance) situation, the subject was probably more focused on the cooperative aspect of the situation, i.e., more attentive to the composite score for himself and the partner in relation to the scores of other dyads. Therefore, the smallness of the difference between evaluations of the confederate in the two Low Relevance conditions could have been due to the presence of these two countervailing factors: the competitive aspect of the situation and the display of high or low mental ability (i.e., positive or negative self-presentation) by the confederate. On the other hand, in the High Relevance condition, the success–failure and self-presentational aspects of the situation tended to work together, thereby producing a more extreme difference in evaluations.

Despite the problem of interpretation, the two anagram experiments of Gibbons and his associates, considered together, are clearly supportive of the ambivalence-response-amplification hypothesis. The studies invite comparison with the investigation by Katz et al. (1978) described in Chapter 8, in which subjects responded more favorably to a disabled confederate who behaved obnoxiously than to one whose conduct was friendly and courteous. How is one to account for the discrepancy in findings? There were, of course, many procedural differences between the two investigations that could have influenced the results. For example, the main response measures used by Katz and his co-workers were the commitment to help the confederate and the covert expression of anger, whereas Gibbons et al. were primarily interested in the subject's evaluation of the confederate's personality. Another difference was that in the earlier investigation, the confederate's pleasant or unpleasant manner had no real punitive or rewarding consequences for the subject, whereas in the research just presented, the hypothesis was supported when the task performance of the confederate was responsible for the dyad's success or failure. Additional research would be needed to establish whether these and possibly other procedural differences between the two studies were responsible for the discrepant outcomes.

SUMMARY

Reviewed were several studies of the effects of perceived stigma and personal characteristics on majority group observers' evaluations of target persons. Dienstbier (1970) had subjects do impression ratings of hypothetical black and white age peers who were depicted in personality sketches as having socially desirable or socially undesirable values, interests, and beliefs. He found a trend toward greater polarity in the ratings made of black persons than of white persons. Later studies by Carver and others, in which similar stimulus materials were employed (fictitious interview transcripts), failed to replicate Dienstbier's findings. In three experiments (Carver et al., 1977), responses to black interviewees were more favorable than responses to white ones in both the positive and negative transcript conditions. Scheier et al. (1978) obtained the same positivity effect with physically disabled stimulus persons. But when a bogus pipeline variation was introduced into the negative transcript condition (Carver et al., 1978), ratings of a black interviewee became extremely negative, in accordance with the response-amplification hypothesis, whereas ratings of a handicapped interviewee remained highly favorable. An experimental attempt to make subjects' ambivalence about handicapped people more salient had the effect of polarizing their evaluations of positively and negatively depicted handicapped individuals; however, the effect generalized to nonhandicapped stimulus persons as well (Carver et al., 1979).

More recently, results that support the ambivalence-response-amplification hypothesis were obtained by Linville and Jones (1980) and Gibbons et al. (in press). Linville and Jones had subjects evaluate applications to law school from black or white candidates whose academic credentials were either strong or weak. To create a high level of task involvement, subjects were informed that the research data would provide useful information for improving the selection procedures of law schools. It was found that black candidates received higher ratings than white candidates when both had strong academic records, whereas the relationship was reversed when the candidates had relatively weak credentials. Gibbons et al. tried to create strong subject involvement in their study of reactions to a disabled peer by setting up cooperative dyads. Impression ratings of the disabled partner whose actions were responsible for the team's success or failure were more favorable or unfavorable than were the ratings of a nondisabled partner.

10 A Nonverbal Technique for Assessing Ambivalence

The ambivalence-amplification theory makes the assumption that extreme reactions to blacks and the handicapped are mediated by conflicting attitudes about these people. Relatively little evidence bearing directly on this assumption was presented in the earlier chapters. This reflects the difficulties my colleagues and I encountered when we tried by verbal means to measure individual differences in attitudinal ambivalence. Efforts of this kind are beset by all of the problems that plague intergroup attitude measurement in general, including what appears (and what the theory postulates) to be a strong need on the part of many people to present themselves as both consistent and humane in their treatment of others. I now describe a further attempt that was made to relate attitudes about a stigmatized group to reactions to particular members.

THE RESPONSE-LATENCY EXPERIMENT

To assess the amount of ambivalence a person may have about a group such as the handicapped, Irwin Katz, David Lucido, Joan Farber, and David Glass (unpublished) devised a technique that utilizes response latency as a measure of conflict in making evaluative judgments. It is a well established finding in research on decisional processes that if there are two competing response tendencies, the time taken to respond will be longer than if there is a single prepotent tendency (cf. Gardner, 1962). In the technique my colleagues and I employed, subjects used a hand lever to make scalar responses to a series of trait labels pertaining to a designated group, and a recording was made of: (1) time elapsing between onset of the verbal stimulus and final positioning of the lever; and (2) the final scalar position of the lever. Subjects were also given information about an individual member of the group who had either positive or negative traits, after which they filled out an impression rating questionnaire.

It was expected that the longer the response latencies when rating handicapped people in general, the more extreme would be the impression ratings of a handicapped stimulus person with positive or negative traits. Latency scores for two control groups (obese people and tall people) were not expected to be related in this way to evaluations of the handicapped individual. Further, none of the latency scores were expected to be related to impression ratings of a nonhandicapped stimulus person.

Method

Men and women were recruited for the experiment through a newspaper ad and were paid for participating. The subject first made evaluative judgments about three target groups: "Physically handicapped men (confined to a wheelchair)," "Obese men (very overweight)," and "Tall men." The two latter groups were included as controls. The obese group was used because it appears to be negatively sterotyped in American society (e.g., Richardson, 1971), and the tall group was selected because there is evidence that it has a favorable stereotype (cf. review by Berscheid & Walster, 1974). Presented to the subject by means of a slide projector and a screen was a series of verbal stimuli in which each group label was successively paired with five positive trait names and five negative trait names.[1] Every time a new verbal stimulus appeared, the subject was supposed to express a judgment about the percentage of people in the named category who possessed the trait, and to do this by moving a lever from a starting point to an appropriate location on a 4-inch horizontal scale marked "0" at one end and "100" at the other end. Unknown to the subject, the time elapsing between onset of the stimulus and the final placement of the lever was recorded. This was the measure of response latency. Also measured was the favorability of the ratings for a given target group, scored as the sum of the ratings (0 to 100) for the positive trait items minus the sum of the ratings (0 to 100) for the negative trait items.

When the group ratings had been completed, the lever apparatus was removed, and the subject was given a two-page transcript of a (bogus) interview. There were three different versions of the interview, each seen by approximately one third of the sample. In the Handicapped–Positive condition, the interviewee was identified as a 19-year-old male paraplegic, confined to a wheelchair. He was portrayed as a college student with high ambitions, varied interests, and many friends. In the Handicapped–Negative condition, the same physical dis-

---

[1]The order of presentation of the target groups was fully counterbalanced across subjects, whereas a single randomized order was used for the traits.

ability was described, but the interviewee was a 19-year-old high school dropout with few friends, no particular interests, and no plans for the future. In the Nonhandicapped–Positive condition, there was no reference to physical disability, and the personality portrayal was the same as in the Handicapped–Positive condition. After reading the transcript, the subject filled out an 11-item impression rating questionnaire.

Results[2]

Correlations Between Responses to Target Groups and Interviewees.   The main findings of the study are presented in Table 10.1. Looking first at correlations between the *latencies* of the ratings of target groups and the evaluations of the interviewee, it can be seen that in the case of the handicapped group, response latencies were significantly related to evaluations of the stimulus person in both the Handicapped–Positive and Handicapped–Negative transcript conditions ($r = .33$, $p < .05$, and $r = -.41$, $p < .02$, respectively). That is, the longer the response latency when rating handicapped people in general, the higher the evaluations of the handicapped person with socially desirable characteristics and the lower the evaluations of the handicapped person with socially undesirable characteristics. Time scores for the ratings of obese men were only marginally related to evaluations of the handicapped interviewees; for the favorable transcript, $r = .28$, $p = .09$, and for the unfavorable one, $r = -.30$, $p = .09$. However, it can be seen that the differences in the magnitude of the correlations for the handicapped and obese interviewees were quite small. Regarding response latencies for ratings of tall men, the correlation with evaluations of the handicapped interviewee was almost significant in the Positive Transcript condition ($r = .31$, $p = .06$) but very low in the Negative condition ($r = -.12$, $p > .10$). Finally, for none of the three stimulus groups were rating times significantly related to evaluations of the nonhandicapped interviewee.

Thus, of the three groups that subjects rated, the physically handicapped and the obese elicited response latencies that were significantly or near-significantly related to the extremity of both positive and negative evaluations of the handicapped stimulus persons.

Table 10.1 further reveals that the *favorability* of the ratings of every target group correlated positively with evaluations of the positively presented hand-

---

[2]Cronbach's coefficient alpha was used to estimate the reliabilities of the main response measures. Alpha coefficients for the response-latency scores were .87 for ratings of the handicapped group, .88 for the obese, and .92 for the tall. Alpha coefficients for the scalar values on the five positive traits and on the five negative traits, respectively, were .83 and .66 for the handicapped, .78 and .71 for the obese, and .75 and .61 for the tall. Finally, alphas for the impression ratings of the interviewee were .80 for the Handicapped–Positive transcript, .86 for the Handicapped–Negative transcript, and .89 for the Nonhandicapped–Positive transcript.

TABLE 10.1
Correlations Between Ratings of Target Groups (Latency
and Favorability Scores) and Evaluations of Interviewees

Target Group and Variable	Type of Interviewee		
	Handicapped–Pos. ($N = 36$)	Handicapped–Neg. ($N = 34$)	Nonhand. Pos. ($N = 31$)
Handicapped–Lat.	.33**	−.41***	.19
Obese–Lat.	.28*	−.30*	.03
Tall–Lat.	.31*	−.12	.01
Handicapped–Fav.	.36**	.18	−.09
Obese–Fav.	.34**	.48****	.26
Tall–Fav.	.36**	.15	.18

*$p < .10$.   **$p < .05$.   ***$p < .02$.   ****$p < .01$.

icapped person, $ps < .05$. In addition, ratings of obese people were related to evaluations of the handicapped stimulus person in the Negative condition ($r = .48$, $p < .01$). Overall, it can be seen that eight out of nine correlations between ratings of stimulus groups and ratings of stimulus persons tended to be positive in sign. This suggests that all of the evaluations were somewhat influenced by a favorability response set.

Mean Ratings of Target Groups.   Sample means for the latency and favorability of ratings of the three target groups are presented in Table 10.2. As revealed by t tests for correlated means, the longest decision times tended to occur on ratings of the handicapped group ($p < .02$ for handicapped vs. tall, and $p < .10$ for handicapped vs. obese), suggesting that the handicapped were the most ambivalently regarded. There were no latency differences between ratings of the obese and the tall. Regarding favorability, handicapped and tall were rated about equally, and both were rated more favorably than the obese ($ps < .001$).

Intercorrelations of Target Group Ratings.   The intercorrelations of latency scores were uniformly high, indicating a substantial amount of generality: Hand-

TABLE 10.2
Latency and Favorability Means for Ratings of Three Target Groups

Variables	Target Groups			Values of t for Diffs		
	(A) Disabled	(B) Obese	(C) Tall	A–B	A–C	B–C
Latency	39.19	36.82	35.41	1.79*	2.38**	—
Favorability	6.14	1.23	5.54	4.36***	—	4.70***

Note: $N = 101$ for all groups.
*$p < .10$.   **$p < .02$.   ***$p < .001$.

icapped vs. Obese, $r = .73$; Handicapped vs. Tall, $r = .65$; Obese vs. Tall, $r = .69$ ($ps < .001$). The favorability scores for different stimulus groups were also significantly interrelated, though not as strongly as the time scores: Handicapped vs. Obese, $r = .42$; Handicapped vs. Tall, $r = .29$; Obese vs. Tall, $r = .36$ ($ps < .01$). Time versus favorability correlations were close to zero, both for the same and for different stimulus groups.

Discussion

The main finding was that response latencies on ratings of the physically handicapped group, and to a somewhat less extent on ratings of the obese, were related both to degree of acceptance of a handicapped stimulus person who had socially desirable qualities and to degree of rejection of a handicapped person with socially undesirable qualities. How reasonable, then, is it to assume that response latency is an indicator of ambivalence?

One kind of evidence is provided by the differences in mean latencies for ratings of the various target groups. Mean response time tended to be longer on ratings of the handicapped than on ratings of the tall or obese. The suggestion that people are somewhat more ambivalent about the handicapped than about the obese, and definitely more ambivalent about the handicapped than about tall men, accords with what is generally known about attitudes toward these groups.

Also relevant to the validity issue is the finding that latencies were unrelated either to the overall favorability of the ratings of target groups (i.e., scalar values on positive trait items minus scalar values on negative ones) or to the total amplitude of the ratings, disregarding the psychological direction of the trait items. The fact that the correlation between latency scores and each of these measures was close to zero for every target group indicates that latency was not an artifact of either extremeness or directionality of the ratings.

A problem with the assumption that latency reflects ambivalence arises from the rather substantial intercorrelations of the latency scores for ratings of the three target groups. These correlations indicate that latencies for all groups had a common component, such as the individual subject's response style in making judgments of this kind. Indeed, it would have been desirable to remove this common variance by subtracting out a baseline score from the latency scores for the respective groups. But this did not seem feasible at the time. But even with the embarrassment of the high latency intercorrelations, the overall pattern of findings does seem to provide some interesting evidence in support of an ambivalence interpretation.

11 Summary of Findings and Theoretical Discussion

SUMMARY OF FINDINGS

The ambivalence-response amplification theory presented in Chapter 3 generates many predictions about people's reactions to members of certain groups—e.g., blacks and the handicapped—that are assumed to be regarded ambivalently in this society. The predictions pertain to situations involving a majority group actor and a stigmatized stimulus person. An initial input of information from the actor or the other person that is positive or negative in meaning (i.e., consistent with either a positive or a negative attitude toward the stigmatized individual) is supposed to give rise to extreme behavior on the part of the actor, either favorable or unfavorable to the other person depending on the structure of the situation. Evidence relating to the theory was presented in Chapters 4 through 10. In order to summarize this material, I now list some predictions from the theory and cite the findings for each. Then the main assumptions are presented along with the relevant data.

Findings Relevant to Predictions

1a. *It was predicted that unintentional harm-doers will be more likely to denigrate a black victim than a white victim.* In a study by Katz, Glass, and Cohen (1973), subjects were induced to deliver either mild or painful electric shocks to a black or white confederate. In accordance with the prediction, preshock and postshock impression ratings of the confederate revealed more unfavorable changes when painful shocks were given to a black person than in any other condition.

1b. *It was predicted that unintentional harm-doers will be more likely to denigrate a physically handicapped victim than a nonhandicapped victim.* To test this prediction, Katz, Glass, Lucido, and Farber (1977) had subjects administer mild and noxious noise signals to a confederate who was seated either in a wheelchair or an ordinary chair. Pre-post changes in impression ratings of the stimulus person showed that, as predicted, the greatest amount of denigration occurred in the Noxious Noise/Wheelchair condition.

2a. *It was predicted that unintentional harm-doers will be more likely to help a black victim than a white victim.* Subjects in an experiment by Katz, Glass, Lucido, and Farber (1979) were caused to make either highly critical or neutral remarks to a black or a white confederate about his personality. When the confederate later asked the subject to aid him by performing a tedious task, the group that had insulted a black person gave the greatest amount of assistance, thus upholding the prediction.

2b. *It was predicted that unintentional harm-doers will be more likely to help a physically handicapped victim than a nonhandicapped victim.* In another study originally reported by Katz et al. (1979), the subjects had an opportunity to perform a boring task for a disabled or normal stranger to whom they had just delivered mild or raucous noise signals. Among older subjects, the greatest amount of compliance occurred in the Noxious Noise/Wheelchair condition; the younger half of the sample did not respond as predicted (possibly because they were less disturbed emotionally over administering the noxious noise blasts). The same researchers did another experiment in which adults were given personality tests by an apparently disabled or nondisabled research assistant, ostensibly for the purpose of providing normative data. Half of the subjects were then told by the confederate that their test responses had not been honest enough to be usable, thereby creating additional work for her. When subjects were later requested to volunteer as participants in the assistant's dissertation research project, the highest rate of compliance occurred in the group told they had inconvenienced the handicapped tester. In the three other experimental conditions, compliance rates were uniformly low. Overall, then, a fair amount of support for the prediction was obtained.

3. *It was predicted that prior helping will have a more facilitative effect on willingness to befriend the same individual a second time when the recipient of aid is disabled as compared with nondisabled.* In an unpublished study by Katz and Emswiller, a seemingly disabled or nondisabled research assistant either induced people to perform a dull motor task as a personal favor or assigned them the task as part of the work they were being paid to do. When subjects were later asked by the same person to volunteer for his dissertation research, those who had not already helped him were slightly more compliant in the Normal condition than in the Handicapped condition; however, the effect of having given prior aid was to increase sharply the amount of compliance to the disabled confederate while decreasing the amount shown the other help-seeker. These results were

closely replicated by Katz and Podhorzer in an unpublished study that employed a different type of prior helping manipulation. (Instead of being induced to perform a boring task for the confederate, subjects in the Prior Help condition were led to write a favorable job evaluation for him.) The prediction, then, seems reasonably well supported.

4a. *It was predicted that evaluations of black individuals who display desirable or undesirable traits will tend to be more extreme than evaluations of whites who reveal similar attributes.* Several investigations are relevant here, including supporting evidence from an early study by Dienstbier (1970) in which students did impression ratings of hypothetical black and white targets on the basis of personality information that was either favorable or unfavorable. Three attempts at replication by Carver, Glass, Snyder, and Katz (1977) used fictitious interview transcripts as stimulus materials. Consistently higher ratings were given to black targets than to white targets in both the Positive Transcript and Negative Transcript conditions. Carver, Glass, and Katz (1978) used the negative condition only, with a bogus pipeline manipulation as an additional feature, and found that subjects whose physiological reactions supposedly were being monitored, rated the black interviewee *less* favorably than the white interviewee, whereas control subjects showed the same pro-black bias that had been observed in three previous experiments by Carver et al. (1977). Apparently, when not on the bogus pipeline, these students tended to fake their responses to conform to what they assumed was a prevailing norm of tolerance toward blacks.

Linville and Jones (1980) had college undergraduates read and evaluate applications for law school from black and white candidates. The applications were academically weak or strong. To maximize subjects' candor and involvement, the instructions emphasized their anonymity and the practical use to be made of the data. In accordance with theoretical prediction, black applicants were rated more favorably than white applicants when both had strong credentials, and the opposite relationship was observed when the applications were relatively weak. This suggests that the negative results reported by Carver and his co-workers for the investigations that did not employ the bogus pipeline may have been due to the use of a weak procedure (the positive and negative interview transcripts).

4b. *It was predicted that evaluations of handicapped individuals who display desirable or undesirable traits will tend to be more extreme than evaluations of nonhandicapped persons who reveal similar attributes.* Scheier, Carver, Schultz, Glass, and Katz (1978) found that subjects gave higher ratings to handicapped than to nonhandicapped interviewees, regardless of whether the interview transcripts were positive or negative. The same tendency was observed by these researchers even when the bogus pipeline procedure was used in the Negative Transcript Condition. Carver, Gibbons, Stephan, Glass, and Katz (1979) tried to demonstrate the predicted effect by experimentally arousing ambivalent feelings about handicapped people in general. Following the arousal pretreatment, subjects read and evaluated the usual interview transcripts for three types of target person: disabled, Chicano, and Anglo nondisabled. As in the prior study by Scheier et al., the ratings were consistently higher for handicapped targets. Although the arousal pretreatment produced greater polarity in the evaluations of handicapped interviewees, the effect generalized to ratings of the Chicano stimulus persons and even to some extent of the Anglo normals.

Gibbons, Stephan, Stephenson, and Petty (in press) had individual students work at a task with a disabled or nondisabled partner whose performance was responsible for the dyad's success or failure. When subjects rated the partner, the handicapped person was more strongly accepted in the Success condition but more strongly rejected if the team had failed.

Thus the one study that used a face-to-face interaction situation produced confirmatory results, leading one to suspect that the interview transcripts may not have been sufficiently involving to break through students' defensiveness about having negative feelings toward handicapped individuals.

5a. *It was predicted that black help-seekers with desirable personal qualities will receive more assistance from majority group members than will white help-seekers with similar qualities, but the preference will be reversed when both types of help-seeker show undesirable traits.* The outcome was only partly as predicted when Katz, Cohen, and Glass (1975) had black and white callers request the participation of urban residents in a brief telephone interview. Black callers elicited more compliance than white callers when both presented themselves favorably, but there was only a slight preference for the white help-seekers when the behavior of both types of caller was less desirable. However, some evidence in support of the second part of the prediction was obtained when subway riders were asked to give change for a quarter.

5b. *It was predicted that handicapped help-seekers with desirable personal qualities will receive more assistance from majority group members than will nonhandicapped help-seekers with similar qualities, but the preference will be reversed when both types of help-seeker show undesirable traits.* In an experiment by Katz, Farber, Glass, Lucido, and Emswiller (1978), men and women were given verbal tasks by a handicapped or nonhandicapped person who was either friendly and achievement-oriented or caustic and apathetic. Subjects were later asked to volunteer to participate in the assistant's dissertation research. Unexpectedly, the disabled tester tended to be rejected in the Positive condition but favored in the Negative condition. A follow-up study examined the possibility that in the Positive condition, people had been annoyed by the handicapped confederate's disavowal of the deviant role, whereas in the Negative condition, they accepted her inadequacies as befitting a victim of severe misfortune. Data obtained with a disguised measure of covert anger supported this interpretation, suggesting that the negative results of the first experiment reflected the fact that actions which are usually seen as socially desirable may not be considered desirable when observed in the physically handicapped.

Findings Relevant to Theoretical Assumptions

The ambivalence theory makes the assumption that extreme reactions to blacks and the handicapped are mediated by conflicting attitudes about people in these categories. Relatively little evidence bearing directly on this assumption was presented. Katz et al. (1973) found that when college students were placed in a harm-doing situation, those with high scores on both a racial prejudice scale and a racial sympathy scale denigrated a black victim more than did subjects with any other combination of high or low scores on the respective scales. Katz, Glass, and Lucido (unpublished) observed that willingness to sign a petition in support of black ghetto residents was related to racial ambivalence as measured by Kaplan's unipolar semantic differential questionnaire. However, petition signing was also related to the component positive and negative scores on the questionnaire, a fact that renders the results somewhat ambiguous. Another piece of evidence was provided by one of the studies done by Carver et al. (1977): Subjects with high scores on both racial prejudice and racial sympathy evaluated a negatively portrayed black stimulus person less favorably than did other subjects.

Attitudes about the disabled were examined by Katz et al. (1977), who found that ambivalence scores on Kaplan's unipolar semantic differential scales for the concept ''the physically handicapped'' were predictive of amount of denigration of a victim by harm-doers. Response latencies when evaluating handicapped people in general were used as a measure of ambivalence by Katz, Lucido, Farber, and Glass (unpublished). Latency was related to the polarity of impression ratings of a disabled person with either positive or negative traits. But other findings from this study suggested that the latency scores may not have been a highly valid indicator of ambivalence. And as already noted earlier in this summary, Carver et al. (1979) were only partially successful in their attempt to show that experimental arousal of ambivalence toward the handicapped would produce amplification of responses to handicapped stimulus persons. Overall, then, the empirical evidence of a relationship between individual differences in ambivalence or experimentally aroused ambivalence, on the one hand, and behavior toward target persons, on the other hand, is only fragmentary and suggestive.

Another assumption I have made is that informational input that contradicts either the positive or negative component of an ambivalent disposition toward a particular stigma group will be experienced as a threat to self-esteem. Bearing most directly upon this assumption are the self-reports of guilt that were obtained from subjects in the harm-doing studies. The theoretical expectations were that: (1) more guilt would be aroused over harming a stigmatized person than over harming a nonstigmatized person; and (2) amount of guilt would be related to post–harm-doing tendencies to denigrate or help the victim. In the four experiments where guilt measures were taken, self-reports of guilt were always higher among harm-doers than among control subjects. However, there was no consistent support for either 1 or 2. But this should not be taken as evidence *against* the guilt assumption, inasmuch as the measure of guilt was a retrospective self-report obtained after the subject was afforded an opportunity to reduce guilt by means of an appropriate behavior toward the victim.

Conclusions

Several behavioral predictions were tested, usually for both black and handicapped stimulus persons. On the whole, the results were positive, providing a reasonable amount of support for the theoretical model presented in Chapter 3. Perhaps the most striking contradictory evidence was the finding by Katz et al. (1978) that handicapped testers who were successful, outgoing, and warm tended to elicit unfavorable reactions, whereas handicapped testers who were apathetic, disgruntled, and rude were usually treated well. This puzzling outcome points up two limitations of the ambivalence theory, as it was proposed. One limitation has to do with a certain vagueness about the criteria for classifying a stimulus person's self-presentation as positive or negative (a point mentioned in Chapter 8). The other involves the fact that there usually is more than one mode of tension reduction available to the individual when a strongly held belief or attitude is threatened. This multiple modes problem also occurs in dissonance theory and is discussed later in connection with dissonance.

As regards the assumptions made in the ambivalence model, it was seen that the relevant evidence is fragmentary. There are a few encouraging signs that individual differences in attitudinal ambivalence are related to overt behavior according to prediction, but there is little support for the view that certain effects are mediated by threat to self-esteem.

ISSUES AND IMPLICATIONS

Arousal as a Mediator

Clearly, there is little direct indication that the observed responses to stigmatized stimulus persons were mediated by threat to self-esteem. One must consider, then, whether a more parsimonious explanation based on the notion of arousal would not be more appropriate. Emotional arousal as a generalized source of activation or energization figures importantly in various accounts of motivation (e.g., Brown, 1961; Duffy, 1962; Hebb, 1955; Malmo, 1959). Arousal is assumed to intensify any behavior performed without determining the *kind* of response made.

Psychological conflict causes arousal. Therefore, in the dyadic situations described in the ambivalence-amplification model, subjects should be in a higher state of arousal when the other person is stigmatized than when the other is nonstigmatized. This is because of the contradiction that will exist in the stigma situation between an initial stimulus event (e.g., the subject helps or harms the other, or the other displays desirable or undesirable traits) and the positive or negative component of the subject's ambivalent attitude about the other. By strengthening whatever behavior ensued after the initial event, the relatively high state of arousal in the stigma situation would account for the predicted tendency for responses to a black or disabled person to be more extreme than responses to a nonstigmatized person. Thus the arousal explanation would seem to obviate the assumption that threat to self-esteem is an important mediating factor between ambivalence and the observed behavior.

However, when one looks closely at the findings in several of the reported studies, it becomes clear that they are not consistent with this interpretation. With respect to the denigration experiments, the arousal view would state that disvaluation of the victims of harm-doing was the prepotent response tendency in both the Stigma and Nonstigma conditions, being merely stronger in the former. But it turned out that only the black and handicapped victims were denigrated *at all;* nonstigmatized confederates were rated about as favorably after being harmed as they had been rated before (Tables 4.1 and 4.3). In the studies of compensatory helping, harm-doers were more willing to aid a black confederate than were non–harm-doers; whereas those who had injured a white person were actually somewhat *less* compliant afterward than were control subjects (Table 5.1). Of the two other compensatory helping investigations, only one produced even a slight tendency for harm-doers to promise more aid than non–harm-doers when the confederate was physically normal (Tables 5.3 and 5.4). Further, in the foot-in-the-door experiments, prior helping led to *more* compliance with a later request from a disabled help-seeker but to *less* subsequent compliance when the help-seeker was nondisabled (Tables 6.1 and 6.2).

Thus quite often the responses made to stigmatized target persons were not merely a stronger version of responses made to nonstigmatized targets; the behavior often did not occur at all in the Nonstigma condition, and indeed in some instances the opposite behavior was observed. These results, then, either do not support an arousal interpretation or are incompatible with it, since arousal is supposed merely to make any prepotent response more extreme.[1]

Other Threat Models of Reactions to Stigma

There is reason to believe that threat to self-regard was a crucial factor underlying the responses made to black and disabled persons, even though there is little direct evidence of this in our research. Rokeach's (1973) self-confrontation tech-

---

[1]By the same token, it should be noted that the term "response amplification," which I have used as a convenient label for a phenomenon, is merely descriptive in a general sense and, as this discussion indicates, can be somewhat misleading when applied to specific studies. The theory states that when a person experiences threat to self-regard over his reactions to stigma cues, he will try to reduce the threat by whatever relatively low-cost means are available in the situation. Often the outcome will appear to be an intensification of a behavioral tendency already visible in the situation, but this is not logically required by the theory.

nique for modifying behavior toward minority groups is based on a similar notion. He argues that for cognitive inconsistency to influence behavior, it must implicate self-cognitions and be experienced as a state of self-dissatisfaction. "It is such an affective experience," he writes, "rather than a cognitive contradiction per se that is postulated here to be the basic motivation for cognitive or behavioral change [p. 226]."

Rokeach's experimental procedure was designed to make white people consciously aware of inconsistencies between their ratings of two values, freedom and equality, and between ratings of these values and attitudes toward civil rights issues. College students were first asked to rank 18 terminal values in order of importance and to state in writing whether or not they were sympathetic to the aims of civil rights demonstrations or had participated in a demonstration. They were then shown the average rankings of the terminal values that had been previously obtained from students at the same college. The table showed that freedom was ranked first, equality eleventh. The experimenter interpreted this finding for the subjects as indicating that college students, in general, were much more interested in their own freedom than they were in freedom for other people. The subjects were also shown the average rankings of freedom and equality by students for and against civil rights and were invited to compare their own responses with these data. By this self-confrontation procedure, many of the experimental subjects became aware for the first time of certain inconsistencies existing within their own value–attitude systems. For example, some subjects discovered to their dismay that they had placed a high value on freedom but a low value on equality; others discovered that they had ranked equality relatively high in their value heirarchy yet had expressed an anti–civil-rights attitude, etc.

At the end of the experimental treatment, measurements of self-dissatisfaction were obtained by having the subjects rate how satisfied or dissatisfied they were with what they had found out about their values and attitudes (general satisfaction–dissatisfaction). They also indicated whether they were satisfied or dissatisfied with their ranking of each of the 18 values considered separately (specific satisfaction–dissatisfaction).

Posttests revealed long-range behavioral effects as well as long-range value and attitude changes as a result of the experimental treatment. An unobtrusive behavioral measure, obtained after several months had passed, involved a direct solicitation from the National Association for the Advancement of Colored People that was mailed to each subject, inviting him to join the organization. More than twice as many experimental as control subjects responded favorably. In another sample, twice as many experimental as control subjects later enrolled in intergroup relations courses. These behaviors as well as the value changes were predictable from the self-dissatisfaction scores obtained during the experimental session.

With respect to our ambivalence model, Rokeach's findings are suggestive. First, they support the basic ambivalence assumption by showing that white college students tend to have cognitive systems that are inconsistent as regards minority group referents. Also, by demonstrating that the cognitive inconsistency involves the person's core values, that making the contradiction salient results in self-dissatisfaction, and that the self-dissatisfaction is predictive of behavioral change, Rokeach's work strengthens the plausibility of the notion that our behavioral effects were mediated by the experience of threat to positive self-regard.

Also pertinent to the self-concept issue is an experiment by Dutton and Lake (1973). They hypothesized that if a white person thinks racial equality is desirable and racial discrimination is not, the person presumably wants to think of himself as someone whose behavior is consistent with these values. Therefore, in an interaction situation with a nonwhite individual who is perceived as a victim of discrimination, the majority group member will operate to reduce threatening cues of prejudice from his own behavior. In the experiment, college students who had been preselected for having very liberal verbal attitudes and beliefs about blacks were presented with information that suggested they might be covertly prejudiced. The subjects viewed slides of interracial and other scenes while their autonomic responses ostensibly were being recorded. Those in the High-Threat condition were led to believe that they were manifesting strong emotional reactions to the interracial slides, whereas the feedback to subjects in the Low-Threat condition indicated that there were no physiological reactions to these stimuli. A check on the manipulation showed that subjects in the High-Threat condition did tend to interpret the arousal feedback as a possible index of prejudice. All subjects were later panhandled by a black or white stranger as they left the building where they had been tested. As predicted, threat of prejudice caused subjects to give more money to the black panhandler but did not affect their responses to the white panhandler. These findings can be taken as additional support for the view that attitudes about minorities are tied to self-cognitions and that a need to defend the integrity of the self-concept can strongly influence reactions to members of these groups. However, it should be remembered that all of Dutton and Lake's subjects had relatively liberal racial attitudes, a fact that limits the generalizability of their results.

The Piliavins and their associates (e.g., Piliavin, Piliavin, & Rodin, 1975) have developed a model of bystander behavior in emergency situations that incorporates the concept of approach–avoidance conflict. The following are some basic propositions. Observation of an emergency arouses the bystander; the cognitive and emotive components of the arousal may include empathy, disgust, curiosity, perception of injustice, a sense of obligation to help, etc. In general, the arousal becomes more unpleasant as it increases, and the bystander is therefore motivated to reduce it. The bystander will choose the response that most effectively reduces the arousal, incurring as few net costs (costs minus rewards) as possible in the process. Piliavin et al. (1975) mention two categories of potential costs for the bystander: costs of directly helping (e.g., lost time, danger, effort expenditures, and exposure to disgusting experiences) and costs of the victim receiving no help (e.g., continued unpleasant empathic arousal, self-blame, possible blame from others). Potential rewards associated with helping, such as raised self-esteem and social approval, are also included in the bystander calculus.

Maximum psychic conflict and threat to self-esteem will occur when the costs of helping or not helping at all are both high—as would be true if an emergency involved a stigmatized victim. Therefore, diffusion of bystander responsibility should be at a maximum in this type of emergency situation. That is, the presence of someone seemingly qualified to give aid in an emergency should more greatly reduce the amount of help given by bystanders to a stigmatized victim than the amount given to a nonstigmatized victim. This effect was demonstrated by Piliavin et al. (1975) when an emergency victim did or did not have a disfiguring facial birthmark, and by Gaertner and Dovidio (1977) for an accident involving a black or white victim. Other reactions to stigmatized victims that are predicted by the conflict model, such as experiencing strong threat to self-esteem if no help is given, have not as yet been investigated.

To summarize, the notions of psychic conflict and threat to favorable self-regard can be found in the formulations of Rokeach, Dutton and Lake, and the Piliavins and associates. But there are also important differences among these approaches and between these approaches and ours.

Ambivalence and Dissonance Theory

The ambivalence model bears some similarity to Festinger's (1957) theory of cognitive dissonance. Both viewpoints postulate that a negative drive state occurs whenever an individual experiences psychological inconsistency between cognitions (ideas, beliefs, opinions) that are held. Also, both theories emphasize that the person will seek to reduce the tension by whatever behavioral or cognitive means are available in the situation. The similarity of our conception to dissonance theory is even closer when one considers Aronson's (1969) revision of Festinger's original formulation. Aronson has discussed in considerable detail the role of self-regard in dissonance theory. He concludes that "at the very heart of dissonance theory, where it makes its clearest and neatest predictions, we are not dealing with any two cognitions; rather we are usually dealing with the self-concept and cognitions about some behavior. If dissonance exists it is because the individual's behavior is inconsistent with his self-concept [p. 27]." Thus threat to the self-concept appears to be a central notion of both theories.

However, the two approaches do not seem to generate the same predictions. For example, there is nothing in the dissonance view to suggest that injuring a person one likes or aiding a person one dislikes should be less distressing than behaving in these ways toward an individual about whom one has conflicted feelings. Indeed, from the dissonance perspective, it might be reasonable to expect that the psychological inconsistency would be more obvious to the actor when an action was in conflict with a single univalent attitude than when the same action contradicted a component of an ambivalent disposition. If such were the case, then stronger dissonance should occur in the single attitude situation. Our model, on the other hand, predicts more inner tension in the situation of ambivalence. The opposing predictions were tested simultaneously in our experiments on the derogation of stigmatized victims (Chapter 3). In the first study, subjects who had scored high on scales of prejudice and sympathy toward blacks in general (ambivalent subjects) were more negative in their evaluations of a black confederate they had just harmed than were subjects who were high on sympathy and low on prejudice (maximum dissonance), low on sympathy and high on prejudice, or low in both scales. In a replication done with a handicapped stimulus person, ambivalence scores based on responses to scales of positive and negative attitude toward this stigma group were related to amount of post–harm-doing denigration, whereas neither positive nor negative attitude scores considered separately were related to denigration. Thus the results in both studies supported the ambivalence prediction but not the dissonance prediction.[2] However, it is unclear whether dissonance theory is inherently unable to deal with ambivalence phenomena of the sort we have studied, or simply has not yet been conceptually extended into this domain.

A difficulty shared by both theories is that of multiple modes of tension reduction. Aronson (1969) has discussed this knotty and interesting problem as it occurs in the work on dissonance. It involves the fact that in a given situation, there is usually more than one way for a person to reduce dissonance. To handle this, the experimenter usually tries to block off alternative modes to force the subject's behavior into the channel of dissonance reduction in which he is interested—e.g., attitude change in the direction of a persuasive communication. Aronson points out that different dissonance-reducing efforts can leave the subject with totally different attitudes toward a target group, ranging from very negative to very positive. He believes there is need to study the conditions that determine the likely mode of dissonance reduction, so that guiding principles can be developed. The same problem clearly exists in the ambivalence model, which

---

[2]In Chapter 4, a rationale was presented for the prediction that attitudinally conflicted subjects would have more need to justify the ostensibly unintentional harming of another person through denigration than would subjects whose initial attitude was one of simple friendliness or hostility. The main idea was that the ambivalent harm-doer, being less sure of the nature of his actual feelings toward the victim, would be more vulnerable to self-accusations of malevolent intent, of perhaps having inflicted more punishment than was necessary. If the initial attitude was unequivocally hostile, the other person would be perceived from the outset as unworthy of concern, and there would be no strong need to justify the harming through further denigration. If the initial attitude was unequivocally friendly, the subject would feel compassion for the victim and perhaps some guilt, but less guilt than if he had reason to suspect himself of gratifying a hostile impulse at the other's expense. Also, an attitude of unconflicted sympathy toward the other would tend to inhibit the use of disparagement as a mode of tension reduction, as compared with other modes such as blaming the experimenter or denying that the stimuli delivered were painful.

predicts diametrically opposite responses to a stigmatized target resulting from the same initial stimulus event. My differential predictions take into account the conditions in the situation that determine the relative availability and cost of different types of tension-reductive behavior. Aronson mentions another determining factor: People should tend to choose the mode that is least likely to be contradicted by objective reality. This factor seems particularly relevant to situations of positive or negative self-presentation by a stigmatized stimulus person. The obvious prediction is that the observer's affective response to the person will have the same sign as the latter's self-presentation (display of favorable traits causing liking, etc.). But even in this situation, the opposite behavior may occur, as witness the results of the "courtesy offends" experiment, in which handicapped confederates were treated more kindly when they were "nasty" than when they were "nice."

Other Theories of Reactions to Outgroups

An alternative to the ambivalence approach to intergroup behavior has recently been proposed by Linville and Jones (1980). Their theory led to the experiment (reported in Chapter 9) in which whites' evaluations of strong or weak applicants for law school were found to be more extreme when the applicant was black than when the applicant was white. Linville and Jones made the assumption that people's cognitive schemas for dealing with outgroup members tend to be relatively simplified and undifferentiated but not necessarily positive or negative in evaluative loading. Because schemas concerning the ingroup are highly differentiated, evaluative information about a particular ingroup member meets the inertia of a complex expectancy and has relatively little impact. Impressions of an outgroup member, on the other hand, may be more heavily influenced by the evaluative significance of new information combining with a simplified schema. Thus, if the information is positive or negative, the outgroup member will be judged more favorably or unfavorably than an identically described ingroup member.

Ingroup schemas are more complex and differentiated, Linville and Jones speculate, because the perceiver must come to terms with a larger collection of diverse experiences with ingroup members—generating a larger number of dimensions along which individual members may be located. Because outgroup schemas are characterized by fewer dimensions and fewer assumptions, new information is greater in proportion to that already known and is therefore more heavily weighted than in the ingroup case.

Linville and Jones report additional data from their study that are consistent with the cognitive complexity interpretation. First, when the individual trait measures used in the experiment on evaluations of law school applicants were factor analyzed separately for white and black applicants, there emerged three factors for the White condition but only two factors for the Black condition. That is, in factor analytic terms, the ratings of the white applicants were more differentiated. This was also reflected in the intercorrelations of the individual trait measures. Of the 120 correlations between trait items, 95 were higher for black applicants than for white applicants.

Two additional studies were conducted to test more directly the major assumptions of the polarization hypothesis. In the first one, white males sorted personality traits into groupings representing traits that belonged together. As expected, men who were instructed to think about white male undergraduates while performing the sorting task used more categories than others who were instructed to think about black male undergraduates. In the second study, subjects read either a strong or weak law school application essay, under instructions to think about either six (complex schema) or two (simple schema) specified dimensions relevant to the essays. Subjects then gave an overall evaluation of the essay. Again, as predicted, the strength of the essay had a more extreme effect upon evaluations in the Simple Schema condition than in the Complex Schema condition.

Clearly, then, Linville and Jones' cognitive complexity theory provides an interesting alternative to the ambivalence explanation of the majority group perceiver's inclination to make extreme evaluations of outgroup members who are presented in a favorable or unfavorable light. Without recourse to any assumptions about the content of attitudes toward the outgroup in question, it makes the same predictions for this situation as does the ambivalence model. However, since in its present form the Linville and Jones theory is concerned only with the effect of cognitive complexity upon the processing of new information about an object of perception, it is not relevant to other phenomena that are predictable from the ambivalence model. For example, cognitive complexity cannot account for the results of the experiments on the behavioral consequences of prior harming or helping of a minority group member. Nor can it explain the relationships observed between post-harming behavior toward the outgroup victim and attitude scores. But even if cognitive complexity is not a sufficient cause of the various behavioral effects I have presented, it may operate as a facilitating factor.

Another purely cognitive theory of behavior toward minority individuals that does not entail assumptions about the content of attitudes toward any particular group has recently been put forth by Taylor and Fiske (1978). They point out that salient stimuli, by capturing the observer's attention, tend to be perceived as stronger, more extreme, and more effective than other stimuli. Since novelty creates salience, a novel person in a group should receive a disproportionate amount of attention from observers and therefore be perceived more vividly—as having more extreme characteristics—than others in the group. To test this "attention-extremity" hypothesis, Taylor, Fiske, Close, Anderson, and Ruderman (1977) used a combination of photographs and sound tapes to vary the perceived racial composition of a discussion group without altering the content of what was said. Subjects heard a discussion group that consisted of either six whites, three whites and three blacks, or five whites and a solo black. As

hypothesized, a solo black was perceived as talking more, being more influential, and giving a clearer impression than was the same speaker when he was
black but not a solo or when he was white. The study was then repeated using sex
composition as the variable. Both male and female solos were perceived as
disproportionately influential, talkative, and prominent—thus replicating the
novelty effect.

The results suggest that blacks, the handicapped, and other minority persons
may, under certain conditions, be reacted to extremely because they are relatively novel social stimuli, hence are highly salient and receive a disproportionate
amount of attention. Note, however, that Taylor et al. did not systematically vary
the favorability of the speakers' self-presentations to see whether solo status
influenced the extremity of observers' evaluations in both the positive and negative directions. Further, it was not shown that black persons are likely to be more
salient as stimuli than comparable whites, independently of the solo manipulation. Even if this were shown, the attention-extremity hypothesis would not be
readily applicable to the full range of behaviors that are dealt with by the ambivalence model. Like the cognitive complexity formulation of Linville and Jones, it
would seem more relevant to the situation in which the personal attributes of a
stigmatized stimulus person are manipulated experimentally than to the situation
in which a prior action by a majority group member leads him to engage in
various types of extreme behavior toward the stigmatized target.

Evidence of Ambivalence Mediation

One of the most important future tasks of research on ambivalence theory must
be the direct investigation of attitudes and their relation to behavior. Unless it can
be demonstrated that ambivalence is a common attitudinal determinant of both
positive and negative reactions to stigmatized individuals, there will remain the
possibility that other processes are at work. Each of the studies reported in this
book was designed to elicit from the subject a single type of behavior (i.e., either
positive or negative) toward a stigmatized target. This means that when attitudes
were not measured and the observed tendency in behavior was toward extreme
rejection of a stigmatized person, the effect could have been created by individuals in the sample who were relatively prejudiced; whereas tendencies toward
extreme acceptance of an outgroup member could have reflected the reactions of
a limited number of subjects who were relatively liberal in their attitudes toward
the particular group.

The efforts that my colleagues and I made to assess individual differences in
ambivalence toward blacks and the handicapped were not entirely unsuccessful
and encourage me to believe that an adequate measurement technique could be
developed. Perhaps what is needed is some combination of verbal and nonverbal
measures, such as was used in the finger movement latency study described in
Chapter 10. Other nonverbal responses such as voice tone, eye blinks and eye

movements, bodily gestures, etc., could be investigated in conjunction with the use of more realistic and involving stimulus materials. Also, projective test materials might be useful for exploring the content of negative attitudes.

Further Considerations About the Attitude-Behavior Relationship. The theoretical model that has guided the research reported in this book can be regarded as a heuristically useful but simplified representation of certain psychological processes. Among other things, it does not take account of differences in the particular formal properties and contents of attitudes toward various stigma groups, such as blacks and the physically disabled; also, it neglects certain asymmetries in the operation of the positive and negative attitudinal components. As regards the latter point, I have mentioned that rejectant beliefs and feelings tend to be relatively unconscious and covert, their expression being in some way inhibited by the friendly, socially approved, sentiments—so that the positive and negative dispositions are not simply conflicting forces with comparable dynamics aimed in different directions.

That the present theory would benefit from a more detailed formulation of ambivalent dispositions toward minority groups is indicated by recent developments in the field of attitude-behavior relationships. Several factors have been postulated to affect the ability of attitudes to predict behavior (cf. review by Fazio & Zanna, 1978). For example, it has been suggested that persons are less likely to behave consistently with their attitudes if situational factors constrain their performance of a behavior or if they believe they are unable to perform the behavior implied by their attitudes. Also, the level of specificity at which attitudes, intentions, and behaviors are measured seems to be important. Specific behaviors apparently are best predicted by specific attitude measures, whereas more general clusters of behavior are best predicted by more comprehensive attitude measures. Another set of factors that may influence the relation between attitude and behavior are the characteristics of the attitude itself. Fazio and Zanna (1978) have shown that the predictive power of an attitude is related to (1) the extent to which it is based on direct experience with the attitude object, (2) the degree of certainty with which the attitude is held, and (3) the clarity of the attitude, as measured by the width of the holder's latitude of rejection.

Any of the foregoing factors may have relevance for testing behavioral predictions from the ambivalence-amplification model. Thus to predict a certain kind of response to a black person it may be necessary to know not only that the target person has just displayed favorable or unfavorable traits, and that the expected response is positive or negative and is readily available to the subject at little psychological cost—but also that the response is either consistent or inconsistent with some important and salient feature of the subject's racial stereotype. In the experiment by Linville and Jones (1980), in which positive and negative amplification of responses was demonstrated, a crucial element of the design may have been the fact that the behavior measure—the subject's evaluation of the academic qualifications of black and white applicants to law school—was clearly relevant to the prevailing majority group belief that blacks in general are intellectually inferior. A different behavior variable, such as willingness to do a personal favor for the target person that was unrelated to the latter's educational or vocational goals, might well have yielded null results. The study in which subjects were more willing to volunteer to be interviewed by a disabled confederate who was rude and apathetic than by a disabled person who was friendly and achievement-oriented (Katz et al., 1978) provided another instance where the interpretation of results hinges on the assumptions one makes about the specific content of attitudes toward the target group. The pattern of volunteering, it will be recalled, was in direct contradiction of the original prediction, and additional data suggest that the anomalous outcome was due to an erroneous assumption on the part of the investigators about the kind of personal qualities people are willing to accept in those who are physically handicapped.

It follows from these remarks on the attitude-behavior relationship that future work with the ambivalence-amplification model must include a clearer articulation of the theory's assumptions about the attitudes toward stigma groups, and about the kinds of responses that are predictable from these attitudes in various situations.

APPENDIX:
Some Thoughts on
the Stigmatization Process

The stigma notion has never been systematically examined for the purpose of uncovering its main conceptual properties and their implications for the study of majority–minority interactions. One finds, therefore, a certain amount of confusion and vagueness attending use of the stigma notion in the research literature. In the interest of clarification, I here continue the general discussion begun in Chapter 1. There, stigma was discussed as an attribute that is deeply discrediting, and some of the ways were listed in which types of stigma differ from one another. But I did not look into the discrediting aspect, the process of *stigmatization,* whereby those who do not possess a certain deviant characteristic assign an inferior status to individuals who do, and exercise various forms of discrimination against them. That is discussed in this chapter.

The reaction of the majority group observer to the stigmatized individual would seem to have two basic components: (1) the perception of a negative attribute; and (2) the global disvaluation of the possessor. Logically speaking, there are three possible ways that the two components, 1 and 2, can be causally related to each other: 1 can be the cause of 2, or 2 can be the cause of 1, or 1 and 2 can be causally independent. Each of these possibilities points to a particular theoretical view of the stigmatization process, for which there is a relevant empirical literature. Thus the first suggests a negative-attribute model of stigmatization, the second a scapegoat model, and the third a labeling perspective. Each is discussed in the following.

MODELS OF THE STIGMATIZATION PROCESS

Attribute as Sufficient Cause

According to this model, certain negative qualities or traits have the power to discredit, in the eyes of others, the whole moral being of the possessor. The discrediting attribute could be any feature of the person's physical makeup, social behavior, or familial heritage that arouses in observers strong feelings of repugnance, disdain, fear, and so on. It is assumed that certain behavioral characteristics (such as might be associated, e.g., with mental retardation or a career of criminal violence) are so central in most people's conceptions of personality, that attribute and possessor are seen essentially as one and the same. Presumably, this perceptual bonding can occur even when the offending trait is physical, and possession of it involuntary. Thus Wright (1960), Goffman (1963), and others have written about the secretely hostile and subordinating attitudes toward handicapped people that normals are revealed to have when interviewed in depth or covertly observed in mixed situations.

The attribute-as-sufficient-cause model also makes the assumption that basic cognitive–perceptual tendencies can strengthen the linkage between recognition of an aversive characteristic and rejection of the possessor. Heider's (1944) principles of naive perception are relevant. His notion of cognitive balance suggests that a stranger who displays a strongly negative attribute will tend to be seen as having other negative attributes as well. Allport (1954) invoked a similar principle when he stated that visible differences between people are "almost always thought to be linked with deeper lying traits than is in fact the case." Heider also proposes that things which always appear together tend to be perceived as causally related, from which it follows that many observers might have a bias toward perceiving the involuntary possessor of a negative attribute (e.g., a permanent disability or chronic illness) as in some way to blame for having the characteristic.

A more extreme version of the attribute-as-cause model has been put forth by Freedman and Doob (1968). They maintain that if someone is different enough from others on any dimension, even one that is generally evaluated positively, he will be considered a deviant and rejected. The nature of the attribute determines how large a discrepancy from the norm will be required to produce stigmatization, but regardless of the particular way in which a person is different, stigmatization will result. Freedman and Doob did a series of experiments in which small groups of college or high school students were given ambiguous, ostensibly nonevaluative, personality tests. In one part of the procedure, subjects were given feedback that their own scores were average but that another person had scores that deviated markedly from the group means. When subjects were later put to work at a group task, it was found that the partners with unusual personality scores were discriminated against in the allotment of punishments (electric shocks) and rewards (monetary bonuses). This finding, while suggestive, does not unequivocally support the notion that mere difference can cause stigmatization. Because there was no check on the subject's perception of the meaning of unusual test scores, the possibility remains that they were seen as being indicative of abnormality.

More recently, Tajfel and associates have shown that even minimal differences between people can give rise to discriminatory behavior when the differences are used as a basis for categorization. In one study, Tajfel and Billig (1974) assigned schoolboys to two categories according to how they responded to a seemingly trivial perceptual task. Each boy was told which group he was in, but he did not know who else was in his group and who was in the other group. Subjects then had to allot points worth money to their fellow subjects, knowing only their group membership. Most boys, it was found, awarded more money to anonymous ingroup members than to anonymous outgroup members, despite the fact that such responses had no utilitarian value for the boys themselves.

As yet, other measures of ingroup favoritism have not been taken, so that the generality of the effect is still in question. Further, it has recently been shown by Wilder (1978) that intergroup discrimination decreases when the outgroup is individuated by appearing to be in a state of disunity. Nonetheless, Tajfel and Billig's results are striking. The phenomenon apparently reflects the strength of a basic disposition, acquired early in life, to assign people to categories and then attach evaluative labels to groupings. In studies of young children's perceptions of foreign nations, Tajfel and Jahoda (1966) found that subjects could agree more about which countries they liked and disliked than about virtually any facts concerning the countries. That there is a fundamental human tendency to evaluate is supported by the extensive investigations of Osgood, Suci, and Tannenbaum (1957), who found that the categories used to classify objects or people have connotative meanings that are primarily evaluative in nature. Any classification label will elicit feelings that may be placed somewhere along a "good-bad" or "pleasant–unpleasant" dimension.

Another line of inquiry that is consistent with the mere difference hypothesis is associated with Hebb's (1949) proposition that discrepancies between expectation (i.e., adaptation level) and perception give rise to primary unlearned affect, the sign of which will depend on the size of the discrepancy. Relatively small discrepancies from expectation are supposed to yield positive or pleasant affect, whereas large discrepancies are supposed to result in negative affect or unpleasantness. These predictions have been upheld for judgments of taste, temperature, saturation of colors, hue, area of the stimulus, sequence of stimulus, and other dimensions (reviewed by Cofer & Appley, 1964).

The Scapegoat Model

According to this conception, a defect may be ascribed to a group primarily as an expression of animosity arising from other causes. As the process is described by Campbell (1967), certain characteristics of the group seem to the observer to fully justify the hostility and rejection he shows it, when in fact the negative reaction came first, generated perhaps by real threat, by ethnocentrism, or by displacement. In the service of this hostility, various differences are opportunistically interpreted as despicable. Campbell discusses this type of causal misperception as it is manifested in cultural stereotypes. But the same point can be made with respect to the stigmatizing of noncultural groups within a society. Thus Ryan (1971) writes about the majority's tendency to assign traits of personal inadequacy to the poor, the black, the ill, the jobless, and other economically disadvantaged groups as a means of defending the prevailing belief that the American economic system is fair and adequate. He suggests that in order to reconcile self-interest with the promptings of humanitarian impulses, the majority are prone to perceive these victims of deprivation as special deviant cases—persons who for good reasons or bad are unable to adapt themselves to the system.

That people will often denigrate those for whose suffering they feel responsible has been demonstrated in several experiments in which subjects were induced to harm another person (cf. review by Berscheid & Walster, 1969). The usual interpretation of this finding is that the disparagement is an attempt on the part of the harm-doer to reduce moral discomfort by lowering the worth of the victim. Research by Lerner and associates (cf. Lerner, 1970) indicates that even passive observers of harm-doing may denigrate victims, presumably as a means of defending a belief in a just world.

Another type of evidence that is consistent with the scapegoat model, as here presented, comes from the experiments of Sherif and Sherif (1953) on competition-induced hostility between groups of boys: Highly derogatory beliefs about the personal qualities of outgroup members emerged as a consequence, rather than as a cause, of rivalrous antipathy.

Research on displacement of aggression also provides some support for the scapegoat model. Experiments by Berkowitz and others (Berkowitz, 1962) indicate that members of groups for whom some dislike already exists tend to be preferred substitute targets of frustration-induced hostility; further, the animosity can be manifested both through overt aggression and the attribution of negative characteristics to the stimulus person.

The Labeling Perspective

According to this model, deviation from a societal norm is perhaps a necessary, but not a sufficient, condition of stigmatization. It corresponds to a point of view (rooted in the symbolic interactionist tradition in sociology) that holds that individuals are disvalued and isolated, less because they display attributes that violate accepted standards than because the majority choose to regard these persons as deviant. Whether a given act or personal quality will be labeled by others as deviant will depend primarily on contextual variables—particularly, the power or resources of the individual, the social distance between the labeler and the labelee, the tolerance level in the community, and the visibility of the deviant behavior or characteristic (cf. Gove, 1975). This perspective, as developed by

Lemert (1951), Becker (1963), Kitsuse (1962), Schur (1965), and others, has been a major influence in sociological discussions of social marginality since the 1950s. [Of special interest has been the question of how being typed pejoratively affects the behavior of those so typed; for example, Szasz (1960), Sarbin (1972), Goffman (1963), and Scheff (1966) have argued that much of the symptomatic behavior shown by mental patients is actually a form of adjustment to being classified and treated as mentally ill.]

Some advocates of the labeling approach limit its application to social deviance—i.e., to acts of law- or rule-breaking such as are classified under delinquency, criminality, addiction, homosexuality, mental illness, etc.— whereas other theorists include such groups as blacks and cripples, whose deviation from societal standards may not involve rule-breaking behavior. How appropriate, then, is the labeling conception with respect to each of Goffman's (1963) three kinds of stigma—bodily, characterological, and tribal? First, the labeling interpretation would seem to be more apt in the case of characterological than of physical defects, because the former tend to be more ambiguous. An ugly facial scar or the bizarre bodily movements of cerebral palsy can function as highly aversive visual stimuli, dominating the perceptual field of the observer. By contrast, a moral flaw may exist only as an idea, an inference drawn from the discrepancy between an imputed act and a societal standard of conduct. Moreover, whether a transgression has occurred at all is often difficult to establish; as Becker (1963) has noted, norms tend to be very broad abstractions that are difficult to apply to specific situations involving real actors. Not only do norms tend to be ambiguous, but there may be several conflicting norms that seem to be relevant to a given situation. Hence, Becker concludes that the characteristics of the audience will be more important than the behavior of the individual in determining whether the latter will be typed as deviant. It would seem, then, that the labeling perspective might be more useful for understanding characterological than bodily stigmas because of the greater ambiguity and lesser salience, on average, of moral attributes as compared with physical ones.

Next, the labeling notion would seem to have a different meaning in the case of Goffman's tribal stigma, particularly of the racial variety, than it has with respect to stigmas of the bodily or characterological variety. For characterological deviance (e.g., criminality), the labeling issue is whether or not the actor will be so typed by society. To some extent, the same question will arise for the person who is injured or ill. (Scott, 1969, has described the social and institutional factors that can determine whether one who is visually impaired will be categorized as blind or sighted.) With regard to blacks, however, the usual issue in this country is not whether a person will be assigned to that racial group but whether being perceived as black increases one's chances of being assigned a range of other labels, such as criminal, mentally retarded, unemployable, etc.

The labeling position has been criticized for neglecting the functional role of norms in a society, which dictates that certain personal attributes and behaviors must a priori be typed as deviant, regardless of who displays them, if the society is to remain stable. Indeed, sociological research to date does not provide un-equivocal support for labeling hypotheses. A book edited by Gove (1975) reviews evidence on the influence of demographic characteristics like race, sex, marital status, and socioeconomic status on the likelihood of an individual being given various deviant labels, when the nature of the deviating behavior or characteristic is systematically controlled. Also considered is the question of whether labeling causes or strengthens deviance. On the whole, the findings on both questions prove to be inconclusive for all of the categories reviewed. But it should be noted that most of the research dealt with legal and quasi-legal processes of classification as they occur in courts, hospitals, social agencies, and the like. The labeling perspective may be more relevant for informal stigmatization processes.

SOME IMPLICATIONS

To summarize, the first (attribute-as-cause) model of stigmatization that was presented holds that hostile rejection of persons who have a particular characteristic results when the attribute has a strongly negative valuation. Next, the scapegoat notion suggests a process whereby hostility—resulting from threat, displacement, etc.—occurs prior to, and is the cause of, the perception of severe defects in members of a given social category. According to the third (labeling) perspective, possession of a strongly negative quality may be a necessary condition of being rejected, but it is not a sufficient one; contextual variables play an essential role.

There is a certain amount of overlap among these notions, and one should not try to differentiate them too sharply. They should be regarded as potentially useful guides in analyzing the stigmatization process as it operates in different situations. Further, they are not mutually exclusive in application to a particular group. Two or perhaps all three of the causal models described earlier may be relevant to the majority's treatment of a particular group. Blacks, for example, may have physical traits that tend to be inherently aversive to whites (cf. Gergen's, 1967, discussion of skin color and race relations), yet there is ample evidence that the relatively low power position of blacks in this society makes them prime targets for pejorative labeling by the dominant racial group, labeling that may be an expression of hostility induced by threat factors.

Thus the likelihood is that there is no single causal process underlying stigmatization phenomena, but rather a number of processes classifiable into three major types. This fact sharply limits the extent to which simple generalizations can be drawn from observations of a single stigma group or interaction situation, although behavioral commonalities across groups and situations no doubt exist.

References

Abelson, R. P., & Rosenberg, M. J. Symbolic psycho-logic: A model of attitudinal cognition. *Behavioral Science,* 1958, *3,* 1-113.

Alessi, F., & Anthony, W. A. Uniformity of children's attitudes toward physical disabilities. *Exceptional Children,* 1969, *35,* 543-545.

Allport, G. W. *The nature of prejudice.* Garden City, N.Y.: Doubleday, 1954.

Angyal, A. *Foundations for a science of personality.* New York: The Commonwealth Fund; and Cambridge: Harvard University Press, 1941.

Aronson, E. The theory of cognitive dissonance. In L. Berkowitz (Ed.), *Advances in experimental social psychology* (Vol. 4). New York: Academic Press, 1969.

Ashmore, R. D., & DelBoca, F. K. Psychological approaches to understanding intergroup conflict. In P. Katz (Ed.), *Towards the elimination of racism.* New York: Pergamon Press, 1976.

Baker, L. D., & Reitz, J. H. Altruism toward the blind: Effects of sex of helper and dependency of victim. *The Journal of Social Psychology,* 1978, *104,* 19-28.

Barker, R. G., Wright, B. A., Meyerson, L., & Gonick, M. R. *Adjustment to physical handicap and illness: A survey of the social psychology of physique and disability.* New York: Social Science Research Council, 1953.

Becker, H. S. *Outsiders: Studies in the sociology of deviance.* New York: Free Press, 1963.

Bem, D. J. Self-perception: An alternative interpretation of cognitive dissonance phenomena. *Psychological Review,* 1967, *74,* 183-200.

Benson, P.L., Karabenick, S. A., & Lerner, R. M. Pretty pleases: The effects of physical attractiveness, race, and sex on receiving help. *Journal of Experimental Social Psychology,* 1976, *12,* 409-415.

Berkowitz, L. *Aggression: A social psychological approach.* New York: McGraw-Hill, 1962.

Berscheid, E., & Walster, E. When does a harm-doer compensate a victim? *Journal of Personality and Social Psychology,* 1967, *6,* 435-441.

Berscheid, E., & Walster, E. H. *Interpersonal attraction.* Reading, Mass.: Addison-Wesley, 1969.

Berscheid, E. & Walster, E. Physical attractiveness. In L. Berkowitz (Ed.) *Advances in experimental social psychology* (Vol. 7). New York: Academic Press, 1974, pp. 157-215.

124

Bleuler, E. Vortrag über ambivalenz. *Zentralblatt für Psychoanalyse, 1910, 1,* 266.

Brehm, J. W. *A theory of reactance.* New York: Academic Press, 1966.

Brink, W., & Harris, L. *The Negro revolution in America.* New York: Simon & Schuster, 1964.

Brink W., & Harris, L. *Black and white.* New York: Simon & Schuster, 1966.

Brock, T. C., & Buss, A. H. Dissonance, aggression, and evaluation of pain. *Journal of Abnormal and Social Psychology,* 1962, *65,* 197–202.

Brock, T. C., & Buss, A. H. Effect of justification for aggression and communication with the victim on postaggression dissonance. *Journal of Abnormal and Social Psychology,* 1964, *68,* 403–412.

Brown, J. S. *The motivation of behavior.* New York: McGraw-Hill, 1961.

Bryan, J. H., & Test, M. A. Models and helping: Naturalistic studies in aiding behavior. *Journal of Personality and Social Psychology,* 1967, *6,* 400–407.

Buss, A. H. *The psychology of aggression.* New York: Wiley, 1961.

Buss, A. H., & Brock, T. C. Repression and guilt in relation to aggression. *Journal of Abnormal and Social Psychology,* 1963, *66,* 345–350.

Byrne, D. *The attraction paradigm.* New York: Academic Press, 1971.

Campbell, A. *White attitudes toward black people.* Ann Arbor, Mich.: University of Michigan, Institute for Social Research, 1971.

Campbell, D. T. Stereotypes and the perception of group differences. *American Psychologist,* 1967, *22,* 817–829.

Campbell, E. Q. Moral discomfort and racial segregation—An examination of the Myrdal hypothesis. *Social Forces,* 1961, *39,* 228–234.

Cantril, H. *Sentio ergo sum:* "Motivation" reconsidered. *Journal of Psychology,* 1967, *65,* 91–107.

Carling, F. *And yet we are human.* London: Chatto & Windus, 1962.

Carlsmith, J. M., & Gross, A. E. Some effects of guilt on compliance. *Journal of Personality and Social Psychology,* 1969, *11,* 232–239.

Carver, C. S., Gibbons, F. X., Stephan, W. G., Glass, D. C., & Katz, I. Ambivalence and evaluative response amplification. *Bulletin of the Psychonomic Society,* 1979, *13,* 50–52.

Carver, C. S., Glass, D. C., & Katz, I. Favorable evaluations of blacks and the handicapped. *Journal of Applied Social Psychology,* 1978, *8,* 97–106.

Carver C. S., Glass, D. C., Snyder, M. L., & Katz, I. Favorable evaluations of stigmatized others. *Personality and Social Psychology Bulletin,* 1977, *3,* 232–235.

Cofer, C. N., & Appley, M. H. *Motivation: Theory and research.* New York: Wiley, 1964.

Crowne, D. P., & Marlowe, D. *The approval motive: Studies in evaluative dependence.* New York: Wiley, 1964.

Crutchfield, R. S. Conformity and character. *American Psychologist,* 1955, *10,* 191–198.

Cuber, J. F. *Sociology: A synopsis of principles.* New York: Appleton-Century-Crofts, 1963.

Davidson, J. Cognitive familiarity and dissonance reduction. In L. Festinger (Ed.), *Conflict, decision and dissonance.* Stanford, Calif.: Stanford University Press, 1964.

Davis, F. Deviance disavowed: The management of strained interaction by the handicapped. *Social Problems,* 1964, *9,* 120–132.

Davis, K. E., & Jones, E. E. Changes in interpersonal perception as a means of reducing cognitive dissonance. *Journal of Abnormal and Social Psychology,* 1960, *61,* 402–410.

Dembo, T. *Investigation of concrete psychological value systems.* Report submitted to National Institute of Mental Health, 1953.

Dembo, T., Leviton, G. L., & Wright, B. A. Adjustment to misfortune—a problem of social psychological rehabilitation. *Artificial Limbs,* 1956, *3* (2), 4–62.

Dienstbier, R. A. Positive and negative prejudice: Interactions of prejudice with race and social desirability. *Journal of Personality,* 1970, *38,* 198–215.

Doob, A. N. & Ecker, B. P. Stigma and compliance. *Journal of Personality and Social Psychology,* 1970, *14,* 302–304.

Dostoievsky, F. *The brothers Karamazov.* New York: Grosset and Dunlap, no date. Originally published 1880.

Dovidio, J. F., & Gaertner, S. L. The subtlety of white racism: Helping behavior and stereotyping by whites toward black and white supervisors and subordinates. Report submitted to Office of Naval Research, Newark, Del.: University of Delaware, 1977.

Duffy, E. *Activation and behavior.* New York: Wiley, 1962.

Dutton, D. G. Reverse discrimination: The relationship of amount of perceived discrimination toward a minority group to the behavior of majority group members. *Canadian Journal of Behavioral Science,* 1973, *5,* 34–45.

Dutton, D. G., & Lake, R. A. Threat of own prejudice and reverse discrimination in interracial situations. *Journal of Personality and Social Psychology,* 1973, *28,* 94–100.

Dutton D. G., & Lennox, V. L. The effect of prior "token" compliance on subsequent interracial behavior. *Journal of Personality and Social Psychology,* 1974, *29,* 65–71.

Farina, A., Sherman, M., & Allen, J. G. Role of physical abnormalities in interpersonal perception and behavior. *Journal of Abnormal Psychology,* 1968, *73,* 590–593.

Fazio, R. H., & Zanna, M. P. Attitudinal qualities relating to the strength of the attitude-behavior relationship. *Journal of Experimental Social Psychology,* 1978, *14,* 398–408.

Fenigstein, A., Scheier, M. F., & Buss, A. H. Public and private self-consciousness: Assessment and theory. *Journal of Consulting and Clinical Psychology,* 1975, *43,* 522–527.

Festinger, L. *A theory of cognitive dissonance.* Stanford: Stanford University Press, 1957.

Freedman, J. L. Guilt, equity, justice, and reciprocation. In J. Macauley & L. Berkowitz (Eds.), *Altruism and helping behavior.* New York: Academic Press, 1970.

Freedman, J. L., & Doob, A. N. *Deviancy: The psychology of being different.* New York: Academic Press, 1968.

Freedman, J. L., & Fraser, S. C. Compliance without pressure: The foot-in-the-door technique. *Journal of Personality and Social Psychology,* 1966, *4,* 195–202.

Freedman, J. L., Wallington, S. A., & Bless, E. Compliance without pressure: The effects of guilt. *Journal of Personality and Social Psychology,* 1967, *7,* 117–124.

Freud, S. [Totem and taboo] (J. Strachey, Ed. and trans.). *The standard edition of the complete psychological works of Sigmund Freud* (Vol. 13). London: Hogarth Press, 1953. (Originally published, 1913.)

Freud, S. [The ego and the id] (J. Strachey, Ed. and trans.). *The standard edition of the complete psychological works of Sigmund Freud* (Vol. 19). London: Hogarth Press, 1961. (Originally published, 1923.)

Gaertner, S. Helping behavior and racial discrimination among liberals and conservatives. *Journal of Personality and Social Psychology,* 1973, *25,* 335–341.

Gaertner, S., & Bickman, L. Effects of race on the elicitation of helping behavior: The wrong number technique. *Journal of Personality and Social Psychology,* 1971, *20,* 218–222.

Gaertner, S. L., & Dovidio, J. F. The subtlety of white racism, arousal, and helping behavior. *Journal of Personality and Social Psychology,* 1977, *35,* 691–707.

Gardner, W. R. *Uncertainty and structure as psychological concepts.* New York: Wiley, 1962.

Garfinkel, H. Studies of the routine grounds of everyday activities. *Social Problems,* 1964. ja211, 225–250.

Gergen, K. J. The significance of skin color in human relations. *Daedalus,* 1967, *96,* 390–406.

Gergen, K. J., & Jones, E. E. Mental illness, predictability, and affective consequences as stimulus factors in person perception. *Journal of Abnormal and Social Psychology,* 1963, *67,* 95–104.

Gibbons, F. X., Stephan, W. G., Stephenson, B., & Petty, C. R. Reactions to stigmatized others: Response amplification vs. sympathy. *Journal of Experimental Social Psychology,* in press.

Glass, D. C. Changes in liking as a means of reducing cognitive discrepancies between self-esteem and aggression. *Journal of Personality,* 1964, *32,* 531–549.

Goffman, E. *The presentation of self in everday life.* New York: Doubleday Anchor Books, 1959.

Goffman, E. *Stigma.* Englewood Cliffs, N.J.: Prentice-Hall, 1963.

Gove, W. R. *The labeling of deviance.* New York: Wiley, 1975.

Gozali, J. The relationship between age and attitude toward disabled persons. *Gerontologist*, 1971, *11*, 289–291.

Graf, R., & Ridell, J. C. Helping behavior as a function of inter-personal perception. *Journal of Social Psychology*, 1972, *86*, 227–231.

Gross, A. E., Wallston, B. S., & Piliavin, I. Beneficiary attractiveness and cost as determinants of responses to routine requests for help. *Sociometry*, 1975, *38*, 131–140.

Haley, A. *Roots*. New York: Doubleday, 1976.

Hebb, D. O. *The organization of behavior*. New York: Wiley, 1949.

Hebb, D. O. Drives and C.N.S. (Conceptual Nervous System). *Psychological Review*, 1955, *62*, 243–254.

Heider, F. Social perception and phenomenal causality. *Psychological Review*, 1944, *51*, 358–374.

Heider, F. *The psychology of interpersonal relations*. New York: Wiley, 1958.

Hentig, H. von. Physical disability, mental conflict and social crisis. *Journal of Social Issues*, 1948, *4*(4), 21–27.

Herbers, J. Decade after Kerner report: Division of races persists. *The New York Times*, Feb. 26, 1978, p. 1.

Hornstein, H. A. Promotive tension: The basis of prosocial behavior from a Lewinian perspective. *Journal of Social Issues*, 1972, *28*(3), 191–218.

Hunt, P. (Ed.). *Stigma: The experience of disability*. London: Chapman, 1966.

Jecker, J., & Landy, D. Liking a person as a function of doing him a favor. *Human Relations*, 1969, *22*, 371–378.

Jones, E. E. *Ingratiation*. New York: Appleton, 1964.

Jones, E. E., & Sigall, H. The bogus pipeline: A new paradigm for measuring affect and attitude. *Psychological Bulletin*, 1971, *76*, 349–364.

Jordan, N. The asymmetry of liking and disliking: A phenomenon meriting further reflection and research. *Public Opinion Quarterly*, 1965, *29*, 315–322.

Kanouse, D. E., & Hanson, Jr., L. R. Negativity in evaluation. In E. E. Jones, D. E. Kanouse, H. H. Kelley, R. E. Nisbett, S. Valin, & B. Weiner (Eds.), *Attribution: Perceiving the causes of behavior*. Morristown, N.J.: General Learning Press, 1971.

Kaplan, K. J. On the ambivalence–indifference problem in attitude theory and measurement: A suggested modification of the semantic differential technique. *Psychological Bulletin*, 1972, *77*, 361–372.

Katz, I., Cohen, S., & Glass, D. Some determinants of cross-racial helping behavior. *Journal of Personality and Social Psychology*, 1975, *32*, 964–970.

Katz, I., Farber, J., Glass, D. C., Lucido, D., & Emswiller, T. When courtesy offends: Effects of positive and negative behavior by the physically disabled on altruism and anger in normals. *Journal of Personality*, 1978, *46*, 506–518.

Katz, I., & Glass, D. C. An ambivalence-amplification theory of behavior toward the stigmatized. In W. Austin & S. Worchel (Eds.), *The social psychology of intergroup relations*. Montery Calif.: Brooks/Cole, 1979.

Katz, I., Glass, D. C., & Cohen, S. Ambivalence, guilt, and the scapegoating of minority group victims. *Journal of Experimental Social Psychology*, 1973, *9*, 423–436.

Katz, I., Glass, D. C., Lucido, D. J., & Farber, J. Ambivalence, guilt and the denigration of a physically handicapped victim. *Journal of Personality*, 1977, *45*, 419–429.

Katz, I., Glass, D. C., Lucido, D. J., & Farber, J. Harm-doing and victim's racial or orthopedic stigma as determinants of helping behavior. *Journal of Personality*, 1979, *47*, 340–364.

Kelley, H. H. Attribution in social interaction. In E. E. Jones, D. E. Kanouse, H. H. Kelley, R. E. Nisbett, S. Valins, & B. Weiner (Eds.), *Attribution: Perceiving the causes of behavior*. Morristown, N.J.: General Learning Press, 1971.

Kenrick, D. T., Reich, J. W., & Cialdini, R. B. Justification and compensation: Rosier skies for the devalued victim. *Journal of Personality and Social Psychology*, 1976, *34*, 654–657.

Kitsuse, J. I. Societal reactions to deviant behavior. *Social Problems*, 1962, *9*, 247–256.

Kleck, R. Physical stigma and nonverbal cues emitted in face-to-face interaction. *Human Relations,* 1968, *21,* 19–28.

Kleck, R., Ono, H., & Hastorf, A. H. The effects of physical deviance upon face-to-face interaction. *Human Relations,* 1966, *19,* 425–436.

Kleiman, M. A., Mantell, J. E., & Alexander, E. S. Collaboration and its discontents: The perils of partnership. *Journal of Applied Behavioral Science,* 1977, *13,* 403–410.

Krebs, D. L. Altruism—An examination of the concept and a review of the literature. *Psychological Bulletin,* 1970, *73,* 258–302.

Lawrence, D. H. *Sons and lovers.* New York: The Viking Press, 1969. (Originally published, 1913.)

Lemert, E. M. *Social pathology.* New York: McGraw-Hill, 1951.

Lerner, M. J. The desire for justice and reactions to victims. In J. Macauley & L. Berkowitz (Eds.), *Altruism and helping behavior.* New York: Academic Press, 1970.

Lerner, R. M., Solomon, H., & Brody, S. Helping behavior at a busstop. *Psychological Reports,* 1971, *28,* 200.

Levitt, L., & Kornhaber, R. C. Stigma and compliance: A re-examination. *The Journal of Social Psychology,* 1977, *103,* 13–18.

Lewin, K. *A dynamic theory of personality.* New York: McGraw Hill, 1935.

Linville, P. L., & Jones, E. E. Polarized appraisals of outgroup members. *Journal of Personality and Social Psychology,* 1980, *38,* 689–703.

Malmo, R. E. Activation: A neurophysiological dimension. *Psychological Review,* 1959, *66,* 367–386.

McDaniel, J. W. *Physical disability and human behavior.* New York: Pergamon Press, 1969.

McGuire, W. J. A syllogistic analysis of cognitive relationships. In C. I. Hovland & M. J. Rosenberg (Eds.), *Attitude organization and change.* New Haven: Yale University Press, 1960.

Mehrabian, A. *Nonverbal communication.* Chicago: Aldine-Atherton, 1972.

Miller, N. E. Liberalization of basic S-R concepts: Extension to conflict behavior, motivation and social learning. In S. Koch (Ed.), *Psychology: A study of a science* (Vol. 2). New York: McGraw-Hill, 1959.

Mussen, P. H., & Barker, R. G. Attitudes toward cripples. *Journal of Abnormal and Social Psychology,* 1944, *39,* 351–355.

Myrdal, G. *An American dilemma.* New York: Harper & Row, 1944.

Osgood, C. E., Suci, G. H., & Tannenbaum, P. H. *The measurement of meaning.* Urbana, Ill.: University of Illinois Press, 1957.

Osgood, C. E., & Tannenbaum, P. H. The principle of congruity in the prediction of attitude change. *Psychological Review,* 1955, *62,* 42–55.

Piliavin, I. M., Piliavin, J. A., & Rodin, J. Costs, diffusion and the stigmatized victim. *Journal of Personality and Social Psychology,* 1975, *32,* 429–438.

Piliavin, I. M., Rodin, J., & Piliavin, J. A. Good Samaritanism: An underground phenomenon? *Journal of Personality and Social Psychology,* 1969, *13,* 289–299.

Piliavin, J. A., & Piliavin, I. M. The effect of blood on reactions to a victim. *Journal of Personality and Social Psychology,* 1972, *23,* 253–261.

Pliner, P., Hart, H., Kohl, J., & Saari, D. Compliance without pressure: Some further data on the foot-in-the-door technique. *Journal of Experimental Social Psychology,* 1974, *10,* 17–22.

Pomazel, R. J., & Clore, G. L. Helping on the highway: The effects of dependency and sex. *Journal of Applied Social Psychology,* 1973, *3,* 150–164.

Rapoport, A. *Conflict in man-made environments.* Baltimore: Penguin, 1974.

Ray, M. H. *The effect of crippled appearance on personality judgment.* Unpublished masters thesis, Stanford University, 1946.

Regan, J. Guilt, perceived injustice, and altruistic behavior. *Journal of Personality and Social Psychology,* 1971, *18,* 124–134.

Richardson, S. A. Age and sex differences in values toward physical handicaps. *Journal of Health and Social Behavior,* 1970, *11,* 207–214.

Richardson, S. A.   Handicap, appearance and stigma. *Social Science and Medicine*, 1971, *5*, 621–628.

Richardson, S., & Emerson, P. Race and physical handicap in children's preference for other children: A replication in a southern city. *Human Relations*, 1970, *23*, 31–36.

Richardson, S.A., Hastorf, A. H., Goodman, N., & Dornbusch, S. M. Cultural uniformity in reaction to physical disabilities. *American Sociological Review*, 1961, *26*, 241–247.

Richardson, S. A., & Royce, J. Race and handicap in children's preference for other children. *Child Development*, 1968, *39*, 467–480.

Rokeach, M. *The nature of human values*. New York: Free Press, 1973.

Rosenberg, M. J. Cognitive reorganization in response to the hypnotic reversal of attitudinal affect. *Journal of Personality*, 1960, *28*, 39–63.

Ryan, W. *Blaming the victim*. New York: Pantheon, 1971.

Safilios-Rothschild, C. *The sociology and social psychology of disability and rehabilitation*. New York: Random House, 1970.

Samerotte, G. C., & Harris, M. B. Some factors influencing helping: The effect of a handicap, responsibility, and requesting help. *The Journal of Social Psychology*, 1976, *98*, 39–45.

Sarbin, T. Stimulus/response: Schizophrenia is a myth, born of metaphor, meaningless. *Psychology Today*, 1972, *6*(June), 18–27.

Scheff, T. J. *Being mentally ill: A sociological theory*. Chicago: Aldine, 1966.

Scheier, M. F., Carver, C. S., Schultz, R., Glass, D. C., & Katz, I. Sympathy, self-consciousness, and reactions to the stigmatized. *Journal of Applied Social Psychology*, 1978, *8*, 270–282.

Schopler, J., & Compere, J. S. Effects of being kind or harsh to another on liking. *Journal of Personality and Social Psychology*, 1971, *20*, 155–159.

Schuman, H., & Harding, J. Sympathetic identification with the underdog. *Public Opinion Quarterly*, 1963, *27*, 230–241.

Schuman, H., & Hatchett, S. *Black racial attitudes—Trends and complexities*. Ann Arbor, Mich.: Institute for Social Research, 1974.

Schur, E. M. *Crimes without victim*. Englewood Cliffs, N.J.: Prentice-Hall, 1965.

Scott, R. A. *The making of blind men*. New York: Russell Sage, 1969.

Seligman, C., Bush, M., & Kirsch, K. Relationship between compliance in the foot-in-the-door paradigm and size of first request. *Journal of Personality and Social Psychology*, 1976, *33*, 517–520.

Severo, R. Cancer: More than a disease for many a silent stigma. *The New York Times*, May 4, 1977, p. B1.

Shears, L. M., & Jensema, C. Social acceptability of anomalous persons. *Exceptional Children*, 1969, *36*, 91–96.

Sherif, M., & Sherif, C. W. *Groups in harmony and tension*. New York: Harper, 1953.

Sigall, H., & Page, R. Current stereotypes: A little fading, a little faking. *Journal of Personality and Social Psychology*, 1971, *18*, 247–255.

Siller, J., & Chipman, A. *Perceptions of physical disability by the non-disabled*. Paper presented at the meeting of the American Psychological Association, Los Angeles, September 1964.

Simmel, G. [*Conflict*] and [*The web of group affiliations*] (K. H. Wolff, trans.). New York: The Free Press, 1956. (Originally published 1908.)

Snyder, M., & Cunningham, M. R. To comply or not comply: Testing the self-perception explanation of the "foot-in-the-door" phenomenon. *Journal of Personality and Social Psychology*, 1975, *31*, 64–67.

Snyder, M. L., Kleck, R. E., Strenta, A., & Mentzer, S. J. Avoidance of the handicapped: An attributional ambiguity analysis. *Journal of Personality and Social Psychology*, 1979, *37*, 2297–2306.

Soble, S. L., & Strickland, L. H. Physical stigma, interaction, and compliance. *Bulletin of the Psychonomic Society*, 1974, *4*, 130–132.

Sontag, S. *Illness as metaphor*. New York: Farrar, Straus & Giroux, 1978.

Sophocles, Ajax. (Translated by R. C. Trevelyn.) In W. J. Oates & E. O'Neill, Jr. (Eds.). *The complete Greek drama* (Vol. 1). New York: Random House, 1938, pp. 315–360.

Stein, L. Reciprocal action of reward and punishment mechanisms. In R. G. Heath (Ed.), *The role of pleasure in behavior*. New York: Harper & Row, 1964.

Strong, E. K., Jr. *Change of interests with age*. Stanford, Calif.: Stanford University Press, 1931.

Szasz, T. S. The myth of mental illness. *American Psychologist*, 1960, *15*, 113–118.

Tajfel, H., & Billig, M. Familiarity and categorization in intergroup behavior. *Journal of Experimental and Social Psychology*, 1974, *10*, 159–170.

Tajfel, H., & Jahoda, G. Development in children of concepts about their own and other countries. *Symposium*, 1966, *36*, 17–33.

Taylor, J. A. A personality scale of manifest anxiety. *Journal of Abnormal and Social Psychology*, 1953, *48*, 285–290.

Taylor, S. E., & Fiske, S. T. Salience, attention, and attribution: Top of the head phenomena. In L. Berkowitz (Ed.), *Advances in experimental social psychology* (Vol. 11). New York: Academic Press, 1978.

Taylor, S. E., Fiske, S. T., Close, M., Anderson, C., & Ruderman, A. *Solo status as a psychological variable: The power of being distinctive*. Unpublished manuscript, Harvard University, 1977.

Test, M. A., & Bryan, J. H. The effects of dependency, models, and reciprocity upon subsequent helping behavior. *The Journal of Social Psychology*, 1969, *78*, 205–212.

Tringo, J. L. The hierarchy of preference toward disability groups. *Journal of Special Education*, 1970, *4*, 295–306.

Uranowitz, S. W. Helping and self-attribution: A field experiment. *Journal of Personality and Social Psychology*, 1975, *31*, 852–854.

Walster, E. Assignment of responsibility for an accident. *Journal of Personality and Social Psychology*, 1966, *3*, 73–79.

Walster, E., Berscheid, E., & Walster, W. G. The exploited: Justice or justification? In J. Macaulay & L. Berkowitz (Eds.), *Altruism and helping behavior*. New York: Academic Press, 1970.

Weitz, S. Attitude, voice, and behavior: A repressed affect model of interracial interaction. *Journal of Personality and Social Psychology*, 1972, *24*, 14–21.

West, S. G., Whitney, G., & Schnedler, R. Helping a motorist in distress: The effects of sex, race, and neighborhood. *Journal of Personality and Social Psychology*, 1975, *31*, 691–698.

Westie, F. R. The American dilemma: An empirical test. *American Sociological Review*, 1965, *30*, 527–538.

Whiteman, M., & Lukoff, I. F. Public attitudes toward blindness. *New Outlook for the Blind*, 1965, *56*, 153–158.

Wilder, D. A. Reduction of intergroup discrimination through individuation of the out-group. *Journal of Personality and Social Psychology*, 1978, *36*, 1361–1374.

Wispé, L. G., & Freshley, H. B. Race, sex, and sympathetic helping behavior: The broken bag caper. *Journal of Personality and Social Psychology*, 1971, *17*, 59–65.

Woodmansee, J. J., & Cook, S. W. Dimensions of verbal racial attitudes: Their identification and measurement. *Journal of Personality and Social Psychology*, 1967, *7*, 240–250.

Wortman, C. B., & Dunkel-Schetter, C. Interpersonal relationships and cancer: A theoretical analysis. *The Journal of Social Issues*, 1979, *35*(1), 120–155.

Wright, B. A. *Physical disability—A psychological approach*. New York: Harper & Row, 1960.

Yeats, W. B. *Collected poems*. New York: Macmillan, 1949.

Zillmann, D., Johnson, R. C., & Day, K. D. Attribution of apparent arousal and proficiency of recovery from sympathetic activation affecting excitation transfer to aggressive behavior. *Journal of Experimental Social Psychology*, 1974, *10*, 503–515.

Author Index

Subject Index